Give Me Your Wounded Heart

A Guide for Confession

D0980958

Medjugorje — A Shining Inspiration

Other titles available from Paraclete Press

Give Me Your Wounded Heart
A Guide for Confession

Slavko Barbaric, O.F.M.

This book was translated into English from the original manuscript written in Hrvatski (Croatian) by Fr. Slavko Barbaric.

Cover Layout: Benoit Bernard

5th Printing, June 1995

Paraclete Press ISBN: 1-55725-023-5
Franciscan University Press ISBN: 0-940535-42-4
Printed in the United States of America

Table of Contents

Introduction

Give Me Your Wounded Heart, by Father Slavko Barbaric, follows his book *Pray with the Heart.* This book speaks to our hearts and is written from his heart. Because the heart is central to our lives, it is obvious that this book will deal with fundamental realities of the Christian life. Father Slavko's first book was on prayer. This one focuses on the sacrament of Reconciliation.

For the sincere Christian, confession is central to Christian living. It is unthinkable to have a Christian life without the grace of reconciliation between God and man. This reconciliation cannot be achieved with agreements or compromises, in the manner of political heads of state. True peace between God and man comes about with the complete transformation of our hearts, which is accomplished only in a genuine, contrite, sacramental confession.

Today, there is a serious problem, because many Christian believers do not understand the sacrament of Confession in the spirit of the Gospels. Often their understanding of confession is superficial and even incorrect. It is not unusual for this sacrament to be thought of as nothing more than a painful judicial court proceeding that simply must be tolerated. When Christians discuss confession, many seem to conclude that this sacrament involves nothing more than listing sins, and then waiting for penance and absolution. Those penitents who believe that they do not sin often emphasize in confession that they did not kill anyone, did not steal anything, nor did they burn anything. They think that confession involves nothing more than saying what they didn't do. Rarely do penitents understand the need to confess sins of omission. Furthermore, liberal minded individuals will emphasize that confession is merely an added burden for believers. They insist that we should confess directly to God, not to His mediator-priest, who is simply human like the rest of us. All of these notions reinforce what was said previously, that the sacrament of Confession is often understood superficially and incorrectly. Before all else, confession needs to be understood as a meeting between sinful man and a merciful God, as a returning of the prodigal son into the home of a good and generous Father.

In a genuine confession, furthermore, we should confess not only the sins we have committed, but also good deeds we have left undone. In particular, because love is the greatest commandment in the law, we need to confess unperformed acts of love towards God and our neighbor. For the Christian, unperformed and neglected love is the greatest sin against the law. According to the Gospel of Jesus, anyone who does not sin against love really could be considered sinless, and yet we know that no one is without sin. We cannot consider ourselves sinless simply because we have not committed any evil, if we have not also fulfilled the commandment of love in its entirety.

The fact is, we are all sinners and we are all wounded by sin. Clearly, one who is physically sick needs medicine and healing. One who is spiritually sick needs healing also, and that healing is to be found in the sacrament of Confession. Confession brings healing and eventually full health to our wounded hearts. It heals our interior sickness. In confession, the doctor and healer is our Lord and God, and the mediator is the priest-confessor. Once we begin to understand confession in this way, then every genuine confession will be more effective and more fruitful, which is often not the case.

This confession manual by Fr. Slavko Barbaric,

which bears the impressive title *Give Me Your Wounded Heart,* is an outstanding directive which teaches how to make an effective and fruitful confession. Even more significantly, in these pages you will find the genuine outpouring of one warm heart who radiates love and encourages you to love. One further observation: whoever reads and prays with this manual may notice that certain sections are repetitious. Do not let these repetitions become an obstacle to your reading. When repetitions are reflections of the flame of love within a soul, as they are here, they are never superfluous.

Though this guide was created for use in Medjugorje, there is no doubt that it can be used everywhere, with equal fervor by believers and priests.

Jakov Bubalo

1

Your Heart is Like a Flower

Recently, the seer Marija Pavlovic said: "Once during prayer, I saw a flower, as in a picture, three times. The first time it was beautiful, fresh, full of color. I rejoiced. Then I saw the flower closed and withered. It had lost its beauty. I was sad. Then I saw a drop of water fall on the withered flower and it opened. I recognized it again in its first freshness and beauty. I tried to understand the picture and what it meant for me, but I could not. Then I decided to ask Our Lady during one of the apparitions. I told her, 'Our Lady, the flower which I saw in prayer, what does it mean?' Our Lady smiled and said, 'Your heart is like a flower. Every heart is gorgeous, full of beauty. But when sin comes, the heart withers, its beauty disappears. That little drop that you saw fall on the flower and rejuvenate it is a sign of confession. When you are in sin, you cannot help yourself, but need help from outside.' "

Dear friend, I am convinced that some of this experience which was shared by Marija is part of your life's experience. Many times your own heart has been like this flower, beautiful, full of joy and peace, ready to bring joy to others and to love others unselfishly. But surely, on other occasions, your heart has been closed, wounded, withered, without joy and hope, without peace and love. Those are always hard and painful moments for you personally and for those around you. And then something happened to you so that your heart sang again, blossomed, came back to life and brought joy to others once more.

I hope this booklet, which evolved from the events in Medjugorje, will help you on your journey, and will enable you to understand how your heart can become and remain a beautiful, blossoming flower, full of freshness; a flower which will exude scents of **peace** and **recon-ciliation.** In Medjugorje, many hearts become blossoming flowers. Many families become real oases of joy and peace because their hearts are renewed and refreshed with drops of the mercy of God joyfully poured out on everyone. I hope this booklet will help you to become eager for your own heart to flower and to bear the fruits of a fully blossomed heart: **love, goodness,**

forgiveness, mercy, peace, kindness, strength, wisdom!

I hope this book will inspire you to work on the field of your own heart, because such labor bears a rich reward. Only the fruits of labor on the heart make a person truly happy. And, if the deepest roots of evil are unearthed in our hearts, they are not to condemn or intimidate us, but to inspire us to seek new life again. Millions of people are convinced that Our Lady is preparing us for new times. She is leading us through her Marian times to the celebration of the 2000th anniversary of Jesus' birth. That is the reason why she has remained with us so long, as she said in one of her messages, "I am with you for so long because I wish to teach you to love." If this booklet bears the real fruit of Mary's school, then no one is going to feel condemned by it, and everyone is going to discover the strength to love God again—God, Who is forgiving and merciful. I have never heard that anyone came back from Medjugorje afraid of God. Rather, many have said, "Now, I finally understand that God is love, mercy and forgiveness." Many who return from Medjugorje love God again—God Who is Father, Who cares for the welfare of His children, Who joyfully waits to embrace us.

I hope this booklet will help each of you to meet the God Who gives life and who renews all things. He cares for His creatures and it is hard for Him if His children are afraid and intimidated. I hope this booklet will be like the messages of Our Lady to the parish community in Medjugorje and to all those who accept them, an encouragement on the way to **peace!**

In light of the messages, we can say that no one has a right to doubt, to despair, to fear, to retreat and not to go forward.

Very often the question is asked, "Why doesn't Our Lady admonish us more? Why doesn't she expose the sins of the world which are the source of all our problems?" The answer is clear. Our Lady is a Mother. She trusts her children. She believes that her children know what is not good and what is not in order. She also knows that it is easier to understand what is forbidden than to understand what can be done and what should be done. For that reason she is continually positive, encouraging, inspiring and hopeful— and she never tires of helping us. When someone seeks after Our Lady in a positive spirit, then the devastations of sin become obvious, and it is easier to decide to fight against sin and its terrible consequences. I am convinced that everyone is going to be able to experience what she said, "If you do what I tell you, you will not be sorry."

2

A Personal Experience

I am certain that everyone has considered the painful and difficult questions, "Why does sin exist? Why are some things forbidden, and some things presumed to be wrong?"

I am convinced that most of us have been troubled by these questions and have thought that perhaps sin was invented to frighten us, to control us and to manipulate us. Somewhere in the depths of our souls, we have probably questioned whether the concept of sin was invented by our elders, our parents, our Church, or someone else in the name of God, so that they can force their wills on us.

It might be clearer if I shared my own experience. When I was in the seminary, the simple question, "What makes something sinful?" haunted me. Although I did not speak out about this question for fear of appearing stupid or even godless, it continued to disturb me deeply throughout all the years of my studies. When I became a priest, I took confession very seriously, yet this question continued to haunt me. After listening and sharing with many people, I began to grasp deep within my soul, that most people did not really understand the meaning of sin. When they came to the Sacrament, their confessions were superficial and routine, and it was very difficult to determine if they were truly sorry for their sins.

As a young priest, I went through a further crisis. I asked myself, "Why do we have the sacrament of Confession?" From the pulpit we announce the Good News. We talk about sin, and we ask people to renounce sinful habits. Yet, in confession, I rarely heard that someone was truly responding to the call of Christ or to the priest's sermon, or was convinced that he must stop sinning. Deep in my soul, I asked myself, "Then, why should we preach? Why should we confess?" I wanted to see the lives of penitents change just a little from confession to confession. But I rarely saw much change and my questions regarding confession became stronger and more painful.

In retrospect, I realize that it is just such questions that begin the tension in many priestly vocations, when priests do not discover the true purpose of their vocations, especially the call to reconciliation. I also realize that many Christians have a difficult time with confession, especially our youth. Then I have to ask again, "Why should we confess to the priest?" It happens repeatedly that many who come to confession only confess unimportant things, and hide the truly important areas of their lives. This has happened to every young man, especially in his years of adolescence. At that time many stop going to confession. Then the priest discovers that those who really need confession are not coming to the Sacrament, and those who do come confess only superficially.

I remember one believer who asked to discuss this Sacrament with me. She made it clear that she did not want to confess her sins, but just to discuss things. Her first question was, "Why do I have to confess to the priest who is simply human like myself? I can confess directly to God." I stood perfectly still for a moment. I felt trapped. I had the same question myself. I did not know how to respond. Finally I replied: "I have a similar difficulty with confession. I have also wondered why we should confess to a priest who is, after all, only human. Certainly, Confession does not exist to satisfy a priest's curiosity or desire to know the sins of others. I am convinced that no penitent says anything really new. The priest has heard all sins, all human acts. I have the same concern that you have."

She was quiet for a moment. Then suddenly we both realized that there must be something more. Surely, the purpose of confession is not simply to expose our sins. There is something much deeper that happens. In confession a meeting takes place between the one who is wounded and the Doctor, between the one who is sinful and the One Who is holy, between the one who has been offended and the One Who gives consolation, between the one who has been humiliated and the One Who elevates the humble, between the one who is hungry, and the One Who satisfies the hungry, between the one who is lost and the One Who leaves the ninety-nine in order to find the lost one, between the one who is in darkness and the One Who is the Light, between the one who has lost the way and the One Who said, "I am the Way," between the one who is dead and the One Who is Life. We talked for a long time, and all the while we were increasing our understanding of confession.

Dear Children! I wish to cover all of you with my mantle, and to lead all of you on the road to conversion.

Dear Children! I beg you, entrust all your past to the Lord, with all the evil that has accumulated in your hearts. I wish each one of you to be happy, but with sin, that is never possible. Pray, dear children; in prayer you will know the new road of joy. Joy will shine forth

in your hearts, and in joy, you will be the witnesses of what My Son and I expect of each one of you. I bless you. Thank you for having responded to my call!
                                                            February 25, 1987

3

Ask and Listen

During my search for a proper understanding of the question of confession and how to confess, I had the privilege to meet with one of the most famous theologians of our century, Hans Urs Von Balthasar. I told him that since coming to Medjugorje, and even before, I had met some people who came to confession because they wanted to respond to the call to monthly confession. Often they said, "Even though I have not sinned and have nothing to confess, I have come to the sacrament." I asked him what I should say to them. He smiled gently and said, "Do not be afraid, Father. When they say they have nothing to confess, thank God with them that they have not committed serious sin. Then, ask them this question, 'Have you loved God with all your heart on every occasion, and have you loved your neighbor as yourself?' Ask this question, and then listen to their answers. Which

one of us can say that he has loved perfectly?
As long as any of us has not loved perfectly, then
we have something to confess and to seek
forgiveness for." At that moment, I understood
the words from Holy Scripture that even the just
one falls frequently.

> Be on your guard. If your brother does wrong,
> correct him; if he repents, forgive him. If he
> sins against you seven times a day, and seven
> times a day turns back to you saying: 'I am
> sorry,' forgive him.
>
> Luke 17:3-4

Even though a penitent says he does not hate
anybody, he probably does not love everyone as
himself, and does not always love God perfectly.
We won't be condemning anyone if we suggest
that no one in the world can ever say, "My love
is perfect. My peace and my desire for
reconciliation are so complete that I cannot
respond to the question, 'Have you loved God
above all things and have you loved your neighbor
as yourself?' " This question is not posed to make
us find sin everywhere, but to help us discover
every opportunity for doing good. We cannot
stress emphatically enough that the main purpose
of Christianity is not to expose sins and to frighten
us. Nor is the main purpose of Christianity to
condemn us. Rather the main purpose of
Christianity is to save us and to heal our sins.

Christianity is the light that searches for the man in darkness. It is love, which delivers man from his hatred. It is peace, which is offered to those who are restless. It is wholeness, which is offered to those who are broken and despairing. It is mercy, offered to those who are suffering from injustice; and it is forgiveness, offered to those who have been destroyed by unforgiveness.

To use an analogy: just as the doctor's main purpose is to cure disease, not just to diagnose it, so too the main purpose of confession is to heal our sins, not just to expose them. As with the priest in Confession, the doctor should not be blamed when he discovers a sickness, but he deserves respect when he offers a cure.

A sick person may occasionally conclude that the doctor is responsible for his illness, but this is unjust and does not help the disease to heal. We can make the same analogy about Christianity, not to defend it, but to understand it better. When Christianity talks about sin and invites us to confession, the main reason is to heal our sins, not to expose them. Once we understand that through confession salvation is being offered, it is easier to acknowledge our sinfulness and brokenness.

We must always remember that Christianity is not founded upon sin and sickness, but it is founded upon the One Who is completely healthy and holy. We must also remember that Christianity does not complete its mission with the sinner, but with those who grow in love and in all the other virtues.

Therefore, my previous questions, and the questions of many believers concerning confession are understandable if confession is understood only as the exposure of sins and mistakes. But that is not the fundamental goal of confession, nor the mission of Christianity. Confession is a sacrament instituted to reconcile us to God. Through confession, man can finally become what he is meant to be, an image of Jesus Christ.

Dear Children! For the coming feast, I want to say to you: Open your hearts to the Lord of all hearts! Give me all your feelings and all your problems. I want to console you in all your trials. My wish is to fill you completely with God's peace, joy and love. Thank you for having responded to my call!

June 20, 1985

Dear Children! I invite you to love your neighbor, especially those who do you harm. In this way, you will be able to discern intentions of the heart with love. Pray and love, dear children. It is with the strength of love that you will be able to accomplish what seems impossible to you. Thank you for having responded to my call!

July 11, 1985

4

The Right Question

Come now, you who say, "Today or tomorrow
we shall go into such and such a town, spend
a year there doing business, and make a
profit"—you have no idea what your life will
be like tomorrow. You are a puff of smoke
that appears briefly and then disappears.
Instead, you should say, "If the Lord wills it,
we shall live to do this or that." But now you
are boasting in your arrogance. All such
boasting is evil. So for one who knows the
right thing to do and does not do it, it is a
sin.

James 4:13-17

In her spiritual writings, St Teresa of Avila notes
that it is easy to fight for good in a struggle between
good and evil, but when we start to fight for better
in a struggle between good and better, the
situation changes considerably.

If we want to understand this insight, then we Christians cannot be content simply to ask, "Do I hate God or anyone else?" Hatred is evil, and it destroys everyone who submits to it, whether believers or unbelievers. Rather, the Christian must be prepared to ask, "Do I love God above all else, and do I love my neighbor as myself?" From Christ's teachings, we learn that Christianity is the school of love. If we talk about hatred, then we are focusing only on a disease which has to be prevented or treated.

The Christian cannot simply ask, "Did I steal somebody else's things, or did I take something that does not belong to me?" Rather, the Christian should ask, "Did I use correctly and properly the things that were given to me to use?" This means that if I can only say, "I have not stolen anything," I have not yet answered the more important question which the Christian must face, "What am I doing with the things given to me for my use?" If I can say nothing more than, "This belongs to me. I have inherited this from my elders. I have not stolen my wealth from anyone. I have worked hard to accumulate what belongs to me," then I am still far from a truly Christian understanding of these matters.

The Christian cannot simply ask, "Do I curse God? Do I tell lies? Do I gossip and calumniate?" Rather, the Christian must be prepared to ask,

"How have I used my gift of speech?" And once we can see that we have not offended anyone, then we are ready to ask the more important question, "Have I praised and glorified God? Have I given others good advice and words of encouragement?"

From our own experiences, each one of us knows how important these questions are. When someone passes us by without saying a word or without greeting us, we feel hurt, humiliated, and offended, even though that person might justify himself and say, "I did not say one word to hurt you." We cannot be content simply to ask ourselves, "Did I destroy my life or that of another?" Rather, we must be prepared to ask ourselves, "What have I done or neglected to do to make my life and the lives of others more fruitful?" The minute we are prepared to examine our lives in this manner, we will immediately understand why we must examine if we drink, take drugs, overeat, or overindulge in bodily pleasures. Clearly, it is not a sin to drink, because God created both the thirst and the drink. But when man is not led according to the needs of his body but by the power of his passions, then he destroys himself and his body. He destroys his potential for development. He blocks and prevents what is positive. He enters into a stage of destruction. Wherever destruction exists, so does sin.

Wherever evil exists, there is sin. But sin exists only in relation to health, goodness, light, and gentleness. Therefore, it is unfortunate when the Christian understands Christianity only as a battle against sin. Invariably, he becomes tired, frightened, apathetic, hesitant, and eventually he loses his sense of Christian mission. Gradually, he begins to live in the world and of the world, and his life isn't any different from the lives of those who do not know Christ at all.

To understand Christianity only as a battle against sin reminds us of the gardener who is so busy clearing his garden of weeds and other damaging elements that he never has the opportunity to plant a tree in the garden. Such a gardener might ask himself the question, "Why am I always clearing and caring for this garden when nothing ever improves? The same weeds keep returning." He may become disheartened, and waste his whole life, or he may give up that part of his work, or even abandon everything. However, when he plants good seed into well prepared ground, and the good seeds begin to grow, he will no longer tire of clearing the garden and creating better conditions for the good seed that is growing.

In a similar manner, Christianity is not only a fight against sin, but it is also a fight for positive values. That fight continues until death and may even require the sacrifice of one's own life by fully giving oneself for others. The real meaning and beauty of the Christian call, the call to discipline, prayer, fasting, and confession, is a call to heroic deeds of love and charity.

The following analogy might be helpful. If someone told you, "God gave me legs so that I won't fall." Certainly, you would not agree with that. You would insist that legs are given to enable you to walk, not to protect you from falling. If people were convinced that legs were simply given to protect them from falling, then they would sit for their entire life, because if they got up they might fall. Ironically, then, the one who sits in one place and does not move becomes a greater problem than the one who is walking and occasionally falls. If we transfer this analogy into our Christian life, we may suggest that a person who refuses to stand up out of fear of falling is destroying himself more than one who gets up and walks, even though he occasionally falls.

Dear Children! You are preoccupied with material things, and you lose, thus, everything that God wants to give you. Pray then, dear children, for the gifts of the Holy Spirit. They are necessary for you, in order that you may give witness to my presence here, and to everything that I give you. Dear children, abandon yourselves to me so that I can guide you fully. Do

not worry so much about material things. Thank you
for having responded to my call.

April 17, 1986

*Dear Children! Live the love of God toward your
neighbor. I invite you to it. Without love, dear children,
you are not able to do anything. That is why I invite
you to live a mutual love. Only in that way will you
be able to love and to receive me and all those who
are around you and come to your parish. Everyone
will feel my love through you. Thus I beg you to start,
as of today, to love with a burning love, the love with
which I love you. Thank you for having responded
to my call.*

May 29, 1986

5

Here Are Gifts

Jesus told us many parables explaining the secrets of the Kingdom. One of them is the parable of the silver pieces, or the talents. The Gospel presents the parable in this way:

> At that time the Kingdom of Heaven will be like this. Once there was a man who was about to leave home on a trip; he called his servants and put them in charge of his property. He gave to each one according to his ability: to one he gave five thousand gold coins, to another he gave two thousand, and to another he gave one thousand. Then he left on his trip. The servant who had received five thousand coins went at once and invested his money and earned another five thousand. In the same way the servant who had received two thousand coins earned another two thousand. But the servant who had received

one thousand coins went off, dug a hole in the ground, and hid his master's money.

After a long time the master of those servants came back and settled accounts with them. The servant who had received five thousand coins came in and handed over the other five thousand. "You gave me five thousand coins, sir," he said. "Look. Here are another five thousand that I have earned." "Well done, you good and faithful servant!" said his master. "You have been faithful in managing small amounts, so I will put you in charge of large amounts. Come on in and share my happiness!" Then the servant who had been given two thousand coins, came in and said, "You gave me two thousand coins, sir. Look. Here are another two thousand that I have earned." "Well done, you good and faithful servant," said his master. "You have been faithful in managing small amounts, so I will put you in charge of large amounts. Come on in and share my happiness." Then the servant who had received one thousand coins came in and said, "Sir, I know you are a hard man; you reap harvests where you did not plant, and you gather crops where you did not scatter seed. I was afraid, so I went off and hid your money in the ground. Look! Here is what belongs to you." "You bad and lazy servant," his master said. "You knew, did you, that I reap harvests where I did not plant, and gather crops where I did not scatter seed? Well, then, you should have deposited my money in the bank, and I would have received it all back with interest when I returned. Now, take the money away from him and give it to the one who has ten thousand coins. For to every person who has something, even more will be given, and he will have more than enough; but the person who has nothing, even the little he has will be taken away from him. As for this useless servant—throw him outside in the darkness; there he will cry and gnash his teeth."

Matthew 25:14-30

What is important here? The man with five talents received five new talents. The second with two talents received two new talents. The man with one talent neither squandered nor lost the one talent. On the contrary, he saved it and returned it to his master, just as he received it from him. But the master was dissatisfied. He took away from this servant what he had received and gave it to another who had more. Now, the one who had nothing does not even retain what he was given. This sounds very strange. You might even consider it unjust. The one with the least, loses what he has, and the one with more receives more.

When we look at this parable in light of confession, we need to understand that injustice on the part of the master is not implied at all. Rather, we are presented with a new understanding of the responsibility of man. Only the one who is perfecting himself, who is moving forward, who is growing, who is not worried even about what he might lose, only he can do something good. He can mature and will be rewarded for his growth. The one who prefers to guard his gifts is committing a grave sin. Whoever does not grow—is falling. "Whoever is standing still should be careful that he does not fall."

From this parable, we can understand why laziness is one of the seven capital sins. Certainly, by laziness we do not mean someone who sleeps an hour extra or is late to school, or who does not finish an assigned task on time. Laziness is reflected in man's attitude towards cooperation with God. If I cooperate in the development of my gifts, then I am industrious. If I do not cooperate in the development of my gifts, I am lazy. If I am lazy, I am never going to become mature, reflecting the image and likeness of God. Lack of maturity represents the most serious resistance to the will of God. God is jealous of the seeds and gifts he has sown in our hearts. He cares about our actions, behavior and conduct. What father does not care if his children are not growing and are not progressing?

What gardener would not be concerned if the seeds from one flower decided to grow only halfway, and not to their full potential? He would become sad and dejected because he had cultivated the seed in vain. Similarly, man was created to grow.

When God created everything, He said all that He created was "good." He also commanded everything he created to "grow" and "increase." That is God's will. That is the divine intention for everything that was created, and especially for man. Every created thing carries inside it the laws of growth. There is no seed in the world that can resist growing when there are proper conditions for its development. Only man, with his gift of freedom can respond, "I won't grow." Man can refuse to grow. In other words, he can decide for laziness. Whenever man indulges that laziness, he is resisting the most fundamental will of God which ordained all living things to grow.

Dear Children! You are responsible for the message that I gave here. Here one finds the fountain of grace, and you are the vessels which convey these gifts. That is why I invite you, dear children, to carry out this work, which is yours, with responsibility, each one according to the measure of his ability. Dear children, I invite you to carry these gifts to others with love. Do not keep them for yourselves. Thank you for having responded to my call.

May 8, 1986

Dear Children! Today I thank you for your presence in this place where I give you special graces. I call each of you to begin to live, starting today, the life which God desires of you, and to start doing good deeds of love and mercy. I do not wish, dear children, that you live the message while at the same time displeasing me by committing sins. Also, dear children, I wish that each of you live a new life, without destroying all that God has done in you, and what He gives to you. I give you my special blessing and I remain with you on your road to conversion. Thank you for having responded to my call.

March 25, 1987

6

The Greatest Sin

Often I have struggled with the question, "What is the greatest sin?" I have asked others this question. I have searched through Holy Scripture. On different occasions, I have discovered different answers. Finally, I think I have found the correct answer. You see, deeds of darkness are only the end result. The cause is much more difficult and subtle to diagnose. We can never remove the consequences if we do not first remove the cause. Now, what I want to tell you is this: All sins are really nothing more than the result of a lack of love. And all the problems in which we find ourselves are caused by a lack of love. Where love is missing, the doors are open wide to evil and to sin. All wars, all family and personal conflicts, all deficiencies, all injustices, murders, abortions, all of them are the consequence of a lack of love for life and for the Giver of Life, the Creator of all. Therefore, *the absence of love is the greatest sin.*

Not even hatred is as dangerous as the absence of love. While hatred can temporarily overcome love, if love is present it will eventually cleanse and heal. But when love is absent there is no hope that things will be eventually healed. Then, the doors to every possible evil open wider and wider. If we look for a comparison, we could say that it is much more serious to be without light and not even want to find the light, than to be temporarily in darkness. God breathed into man's heart not only the gift of love, but also the deep desire to be loved and to be accepted by others. None of us is indifferent to whether others like us or dislike us.

In Baptism, we were given the divine seeds of faith, hope, and love as gifts. Through Baptism, God prepares the soil so that these seeds can grow and develop. When these seeds mature, when we cultivate their growth and development, we become the image and likeness of the Father. If we are not committed to doing this, then love, faith and hope are left only as seeds and the talent remains wrapped up and hidden, not necessarily destroyed but unused.

When we fail to cultivate love, we commit the first fundamental sin, which is the starting point for all other sins, all troubles and all destruction! If we are not working every day to cultivate our love, then spiritual death is already present and with it will come all other evils.

Nothing is more essential for man than to be committed to growing in love. With this commitment, he will do everything possible to develop love toward himself, toward God, toward his neighbor, and toward all creatures. This love will make him strong, and he will eventually stop living according to the standards of the world. On the other hand, as long as love is dependent on being loved in return, it is immature love. As long as we calculate whether or not to return love in the same measure we have received it, or if we say, "If I am not loved then I am not going to love," then our love is conditional. Then our love is no different from the love of pagans who know how to love those who love them and lend to those from whom they hope to receive in return. However, when we are committed to love and determined to do everything to make our love steadfast, then we become capable of the most beautiful acts in the world and we learn the only right and effective way to defeat death and destruction—which means we learn how to defeat sin.

With this kind of love, it is not hard to imagine all wars coming to an end, the hungry having food, the sick being treated with dignity, the rejected having someone to accept them, the persecuted being honored with freedom, the sad becoming joyful, and the wounded becoming cured and healthy. Only love can accomplish this. If we are not convinced of this now, and do not even dare to dream such a dream, it is only a sign that we have not understood what love can accomplish. It is the same love that has been poured out into our hearts, as Saint Paul teaches in Romans 5:5. Without love, all interior and exterior pains will overcome man and destroy him. And the greatest threat to love is sin, because regardless of the kind of sin, its presence always chokes love in the heart.

7

Love Loved

But I shall show you a still more excellent way: If I speak in human and angelic tongues but do not have love, I am a resounding gong or a clashing cymbal. And if I have the gift of prophecy and comprehend all mysteries and all knowledge; If I have all faith so as to move mountains but do not have love, I am nothing. If I give away everything I own, and if I hand my body over so that I may boast but do not have love, I gain nothing. Love is patient, love is kind. It is not jealous, it is not pompous, it is not inflated, it is not rude, it does not seek its own interests, it is not quick tempered, it does not brood over injury, it does not rejoice over wrongdoing but rejoices with the truth. It bears all things, believes all things, hopes all things, endures all things. Love never fails. If there are prophecies, they will be brought to nothing;

if tongues, they will cease; if knowledge, it will be brought to nothing. For we know partially, and we prophesy partially, but when the perfect comes, the partial will pass away. When I was a child, I used to talk like a child, think as a child, reason as a child; when I became a man, I put away childish things. At present we see indistinctly, as in a mirror, but then we shall see face to face. At present I know only partially; then I shall know fully, as I am fully known. Only three things endure: faith, hope and love; but the greatest of these is love.

I Corinthians 13:1-13

"I am not afraid to be judged for what I have done, but for what I could have done." *(Patrick Lennan, Bishop)*

Without any merit on our part, God's love enters into our hearts. The world, on the other hand, is entangled in evil, conflicts, hatred, and many other things. There is no person or system that can cut the Gordian Knot of the disorder of this world. That can only be cut with a divine sword, carried by a divine hand, and sharpened with divine strength. This is **God's love.** Without any merit on our part, that love is poured into our hearts. Saint John tells us, "We, for our part, love because He first loved us" (I John 4:19).

God's love for us is both a guarantee and a prerequisite for the development of our love. Christianity offers man the unique possibility to grow in perfection, and in the end to become completely perfect. Therefore, we can say that Christianity does not seek man to make him perfect. Rather, man seeks Christianity so that he can love with the love of God which is already poured into his heart. Once man believes in this seed of love which is planted in the garden of his soul, then he will be determined to do everything possible to make this love grow. That effort is merely cooperation with divine love which both plants the seed and gives growth to love in man.

8

Sacred Flame

I believe it will be helpful to read the following story. Read it calmly, the way it unfolds here. I think it will help you to understand better and it will be useful for the continuation of our meditation.

This story took place in the newborn republic of Firence. The name of our hero is Raniero Ranieri.

Raniero journeyed with the Crusaders to capture the grave of Christ in Jerusalem. He was proud of his strength. He and Gotfrid Bulonjskog were the first ones to surmount the walls of Jerusalem. As a result, that same evening, Raniero was privileged to light the candle he was carrying from the flame of the candle burning on Christ's grave.

Unfortunately for most of the crusaders, the liberation of Jerusalem became an occasion for plundering and violence. And, according to the tales of a minstrel who went from tent to tent entertaining that evening, many pilgrims murdered and robbed even before they left their homes. The minstrel in Raniero's tent narrated his tales with such skill and fascination, that Raniero vowed to bring the flame of his candle single handedly to Firence. Surrounded by laughing and drunken knights, he insisted that he would accomplish the impossible.

Because Raniero was by nature wild and aggressive, he quickly became like all the other pilgrims. At dawn, he secretly took the candle which he had lighted on Christ's grave and started through the fog, on his long trip toward Firence. He put on a pilgrim's cloak in order to protect the flame from the wind. Soon, it became obvious that the flame would go out if he rode his horse quickly. Yet, his war horse was unaccustomed to going slowly. So, Raniero rode facing backwards to protect the flame with his chest, from the wind of the ride.

As he reached the desert, robbers attacked him. They were the discontented and troubled people who harassed the armies. Raniero had the skill to disperse hundreds of such robbers, but he was afraid that if he tried, the flame of the candle would go out. Consequently, he offered them everything that he had. He offered his suit, his horse and his arms, and he asked them to leave him only his candle and let him go in peace. They welcomed his offer because they were exhausted from fighting. They took everything except some candles he was carrying, his pilgrim cloak and the lighted candle. Then, they mounted him on an old horse in exchange for his fine, white horse, and left.

At this point, Raniero began to have serious misgivings about himself. He thought that he was no longer behaving like a knight, the leader of the glorious crusaders, but rather like a crazy beggar. Perhaps he should abandon this venture. He had no idea what else might happen because of the flame?

Nevertheless, he did not give up. During his journey he experienced all kinds of humiliation and suffering. Even his own countrymen, pilgrims on their way to Jerusalem, taunted him in his native tongue and yelled out, "Fool!" Angry shepherds attacked him, even though he was only trying to protect the flame.

On another occasion, he spent a night's rest in a place where caravans of pilgrims and merchants were lodged. Even though the place was crowded, the owner found room for Raniero and his horse. Raniero mused to himself, "This man took pity on me. If I still had my expensive garments and my white horse, it would be harder to travel through this land. I am beginning to think that the robbers did me a great favor."

He was so exhausted that evening that he did nothing more to protect the candle than put some stones around it to make it stand upright. And, even though he intended to keep a vigil over the flame, he dropped on to the straw and fell asleep.

On awakening in the morning, he immediately wondered what had happened to the flame? The candle was not in the place where he had left it the previous night. He almost felt relieved to think that if the candle were gone he could end his mission. Yet, he was not genuinely relieved. He doubted that he could now return to his former, violent lifestyle. And, at the moment he was thinking these thoughts, the owner of the lodge appeared carrying the candle. The owner told him that he had guarded the flame throughout the night because he understood how important it was to keep the light burning. Raniero was overjoyed. He took the candle and continued on his journey.

As he went on, he was proud of the flame, but sometimes he had misgivings about guarding and protecting it. When it rained while he was going through the Lebanon mountains, he hid in caves to protect the flame. Once he almost froze. Yet, because he did not want to use the flame of the candle to light a fire to warm himself, he hid the candle in a Saracen grave. Then, after he had begun to freeze, lightning struck a tree and started a fire. And this is how he came to have a fire, but he never used the sacred flame to start it. Eventually, events like these no longer surprised him.

In the vicinity of Nicea, he met up with some oriental knights and among them was one famous traveling knight and troubadour. When these knights saw how Raniero was seated backwards in the saddle with his old pilgrim's cloak, his overgrown beard and his lighted candle in his hands, they began to mock him and cry out, "Fool, fool."

The knight troubadour signaled them to be quiet. Then he came to Raniero and asked him from where he was traveling. "From Jerusalem, Sir," responded Raniero humbly.

"Your candle was not extinguished on the journey?" "The flame burning on this candle is the same one I lighted on Christ's grave," responded Raniero. Then the troubadour knight said, "I too am carrying only a single flame. And I would like to see my flame burn perpetually.

Tell me, since you have succeeded in carrying your flame all the way from Jerusalem, what should I do to protect my flame so that it will not go out?"

"Sir," said Raniero, "it is a very difficult undertaking, even though it sounds easy. This small flame requires your complete attention. You cannot think about anything else. It will not let you have a mistress, if you have such an inclination. When you are guarding the flame, you cannot even relax at table with your friends. Nothing can occupy your mind except protecting this flame. Nothing else can be more important to you. But the main reason why I would tell you not to follow my example, and why I would advise you against such an undertaking is that you can never be confident that you will succeed in carrying the flame to your goal. Never for one moment will you be certain. You must always be prepared to have the flame stolen from you at any moment." That was Raniero's answer. But Robert, the troubadour, proudly raised his head and said, "What you did for your flame, I will do for mine."

After this incident, the rest of the story continues in Italy. Raniero was riding on a lonely road over a hill, when suddenly a woman ran after him begging for the flame of his candle. She called out to him saying, "The fire in my kitchen has gone out, and my children are hungry. Lend me your candle, please, so that I can light my oven and bake bread for my children." Then she reached out with her hand for the candle. But Raniero pulled the candle away because he wanted the sacred flame of his candle to be used first to light the candle on the altar of the Blessed Virgin Mary in his parish church in Firence. The woman then cried out, "Please, pilgrim, lend me the flame because the life of my children is at stake. Their life is the flame that I am responsible for." These words touched Raniero deeply and he relented, and allowed her to light her candle from his sacred flame.

A few hours later, in a small village, a peasant threw Raniero a cloak as a gesture of kindness. But the cloak accidentally fell on his candle and extinguished the flame. Suddenly, Raniero recalled the woman who, a few hours earlier, had lighted her candle from his flame. Immediately, he returned to her home and from her fireplace he relighted the flame of his candle.

Then he began to ride between the blue hills close to Firence. He was thinking that soon his journey with the flame would be completed. He began to remember the spoils of war, and the crusaders in Jerusalem who were probably startled by his disappearance. It suddenly became apparent to him that he was no longer attracted by the adventurous thoughts of war. He quickly realized that he was not the same man who had set out from the walls of the Sacred City. Now, he found pleasure only in those things which brought peace, gentleness, prudence.

Finally, near Easter, Raniero reached Firence. Ironically, now that he had reached his goal, his worst sufferings began. No sooner had he passed through the city gate than the scoundrels and loafers of the city ran after him, yelling loudly. They tried to extinguish his candle. But Raniero lifted it high to protect it from the mad crowd. They were throwing their hats and blowing with all their strength in the direction of the candle, trying to extinguish it. The scene was silly and pathetic. Raniero truly looked like a fool. The crowd was overjoyed with this rude entertainment. Many faces gaped out from the windows and the people enjoyed the entertainment. Raniero looked pathetic. He rose up in the saddle, trying to defend the flame. One woman, from a low balcony, snatched the candle from his hand and ran with it into her house. Everyone was overcome with laughter and jubilation. Raniero thrashed in his saddle and fell to the ground. Within a second, the street was deserted and empty.

Then, out of the house ran Francesca, Raniero's wife, carrying the lighted candle. She was the one who had taken his candle from the balcony, intending to help him save the flame. When the light of the candle fell on Raniero's face, he moved and opened his eyes. Francesca handed the flame to him. He did not realize she was his wife because he had not taken his eyes off the flame. Because he insisted on carrying the flame into the Cathedral, she helped him into his saddle. Although she knew he was her husband, she thought he must be crazy because he did not take his attention from the flame. Then, startled by the woman's cry, Raniero suddenly looked and recognized that it was his own wife who was leading him into the cathedral. Realizing that she was the one who had saved his flame, he gazed at her for a moment, but did not speak to her.

Carrying the sacred flame, he began moving toward the shrine. Quickly, the news spread that the knight Raniero Ranieri had come from Jerusalem carrying the sacred flame which he has kindled from the flame on Christ's grave. Francesca, his wife, suddenly found herself delivered from a hopeless and miserable situation and experienced great happiness. But then, the voices of taunters arose, especially those who had previously been hurt by Raniero's brash behavior. They asked Raniero to prove that he had actually accomplished all that he claimed.

Raniero was afraid. He was not prepared for this. "Whom shall I call for witnesses?" he asked.

"Not one shield-bearer accompanied me. The deserts and mountains are my only witnesses."

Suddenly, there was such a great commotion in the church that Raniero was afraid that now, as he came so close to the altar, the flame of his candle might go out. At that moment a bird, frightened and confused, entered through the open door of the church and hit the candle. The flame went out. Raniero's hands lost their strength, and his eyes filled with tears. Then, suddenly, throughout the church, there arose shouts of jubilation from all the onlookers because the bird's wings had become inflamed from the Sacred Flame. The bird flew, desperately chirping, and then fell on to the altar. But, before the flame from the bird's wings was extinguished, Raniero approached with his candle and lighted it from the flame which was smoldering. This was the proof that the crowd was seeking.

Since that time, Raniero has become the protector of widows and orphans. He has lived peacefully and happily with Francesca, and his countrymen have respected and loved him. In remembrance of all his undertakings, Raniero has been named pazzo di Raniero, "crazy Raniero," and that has become the nickname for his descendants.

Vesna Krmpotic,
Shirt of the Happy Man, pages 114-118,
Zagreb, 1989

From this story the following is clear: The knight was inspired by the flame lighted on Christ's grave, and afterwards no challenge was too difficult for him to protect that flame and bring it into his country. There was no obstacle that he would not overcome. Whenever he met situations that he didn't know how to handle, inevitably things worked out in his favor because his intentions were good and sincere. Afterwards, it was not difficult for him to give up his life of knighthood and warfare, all to carry his flame in peace. Previous temptations to live a life just for material values left him because he had renounced them. From within himself, old pride sometimes tempted him, and old friends doubted the truth of his story and insisted he was crazy. In the end, everything was renewed.

To apply this story to Christianity means simply that we must be committed to grow in love, peace, justice and mercy, and be prepared to sacrifice everything for them. How many times have little things kept us apart from one another? How often have old pride and arrogance choked the flame of our love? How much do we suffer because of our lack of love? We quarrel, and it all looks so normal to us. But, it brings real damage.

9

Work on the Heart

When we hear Our Lady's call to work on our hearts as on a field, we understand easily what she wants us to do and how she wants us to do it. Whoever has worked in a field knows from experience that even a divine seed will bear no fruit unless the field has been properly prepared. We labor in vain if we do not remove the roots of weeds completely. Otherwise, the weeds will grow and choke even the best seed. A careless gardener, who only occasionally visits his vineyard or his field, will never have an abundant yield. Whereas, the gardener who conscientiously clears and prepares the field and cares for the plants will have an abundant yield.

It is equally important for the Christian to work diligently to cultivate the life of his heart, and to use all his resources to accomplish this. Man is not put off by the difficulty of any labor once he understands its meaning and purpose. The Christian, too, will work tirelessly and even endure great suffering in order to produce the most beautiful fruit, which is love.

It is our human nature to work tirelessly and relentlessly once we are inspired by an ideal. On the other hand, when we cannot find meaning in our work, our efforts are usually apathetic and halfhearted. Man definitely has the determination and strength to overcome his problems. But the challenge is to discover what will mobilize this strength.

Deep within his soul, man is constantly searching for love, even though he often sins and shows hatred towards others and appears to be working against love. Man never degenerates to the point that he is indifferent to receiving love or hate, acceptance or rejection, affection or aloofness, joy or sorrow, respect or contempt. This searching is the reason why Christianity always attracts man, in any time and in any situation. From the depths of his being, man is always seeking love and peace. For this reason, the human heart is such good soil for Christian seed, even though producing real fruit always involves clearing, pruning and sowing new seeds of divine life.

Therefore, it is necessary to understand the value of pruning plants. If we have never pruned plants, we might wonder why they are pruned. After all, pruning initially appears to damage and hurt the plant. Yet we all know what our vineyards and plants would be like if we did not prune them.

The laws of human growth and the development of Christian values are similar to the laws of growing and ripening that we observe in nature. Whenever man purifies himself of sin, he awakens new life within himself, and by awakening this new life within himself, he grows deeply and matures. If man refuses to purify himself of sin, he will not grow. Whenever this happens, man begins to destroy himself. Eventually, he destroys not only himself, but also his family and ultimately his entire community.

This work on the spiritual fields of our human hearts is deeply connected to the real meaning of our lives. The more we invest in our spiritual growth, the happier we become. We become more peaceful and more content. Eventually, it is easier for us to use all our power and strength to become spiritually mature. Then, we are finally on the way to understanding the real meaning of our lives.

On the other hand, when we neglect our spiritual growth, and discover neither the real meaning of our lives nor the meaning of our efforts, then everything we do becomes meaningless. The more we live this way, the more our lives fill up with pain and suffering. The more our lives fill up with pain and suffering, the more we run away from ourselves and from others. Because of this, we must say, "Work on your heart and live. If you do not work on your heart, you will die."

Dear Children! Everything has its own time. Today I call you to start working on your hearts. Now that all the work in the fields is over, you are finding time for cleaning even the most neglected areas, but you leave your heart aside. Work more and clean with love every part of your heart. Thank you for having responded to my call.

October 17, 1985

Dear Children! Today I wish to tell you to begin to work in your hearts as you are working in the fields. Work and change your hearts so that a new spirit from God can take its place in your hearts. Thank you for having responded to my call.

April 25, 1985

10

Who Sets the Measures

And Jesus went to the Mount of Olives. But early in the morning he arrived again in the temple area, and all the people started coming to him, and he sat down and taught them. Then the scribes and the Pharisees brought a woman who had been caught in adultery and made her stand in the middle. They said to him, "Teacher, this woman was caught in the very act of committing adultery. Now in the law, Moses commanded us to stone such women. So what do you say?" They said this to test him, so that they could have some charge to bring against him. Jesus bent down and began to write on the ground with his finger. But when they continued asking him, he straightened up and said to them, "Let the one among you who is without sin be the first to throw a stone at her." Again he bent down and wrote on the ground. And in response, they went away one by one, beginning with the elders. So he was left alone with the woman before him. Then Jesus straightened up and said to her, "Woman, where are they? Has no one condemned you?" She replied, "No one, sir." Then Jesus said, "Neither do I condemn you. Go, and from now on do not sin any more."

John 8:1-12

The questions we might ask at this point are: "Why was man created? What is the real purpose of his life? How is he meant to develop in order to become fully human? Who sets the ultimate standards for man's development? Is it his parents, his family, the Church, the nation, or the secular community?" When the family, or parents, or the community or some other person starts setting rules and limits for one another, isn't that when all the conflicts begin, leading eventually to divorces, murders, persecutions and even imprisonments? Does not the rebelliousness of youth begin when the adolescent asks, "Why should anyone set limits for me and direct my growth?" The real answer to this question is that no person can set a measure or determine a path for any other person. It cannot be done by parents, the family, the government, or the larger community.

Man's real purpose and destiny lie deep within his soul, and all efforts to influence and form man must be in service to that fundamental purpose.

Parents are not entitled to raise their children just to conform to their own desires. Rather, parents are obligated to raise them to become independent and mature adults. Systems and governments may not subordinate individuals to their own ends. Rather, they must enable all people to recognize and to develop their own individual talents, especially their innate capacity for freedom, justice and mercy.

When individuals, systems, families, and communities try to suppress man and to subordinate him to their own purposes and goals, man becomes an object, a mere instrument, and he inevitably begins growing in the wrong direction. Once man begins growing in the wrong direction, all that he influences becomes corrupt. It is the responsibility of every government, of every educational institution, of every family, of everyone influencing the individual, to help man grow in the right direction, to help him become fully human and fully mature. A truly mature person will carry out his responsibilities, and will help protect his own rights and the rights of others.

As man struggles to find his place within his community and his family, he can become selfish and willful. When this happens, he is just as lost as if he grew only according to the expectations of others.

In any case, man was created neither to govern his own behavior autonomously, nor to be governed autonomously by others. The fundamental reason and purpose of man's life is for him to become mature in love. Every influence over man must be subordinated to that fundamental goal. Once this is accomplished, there will emerge a right ordering of relationships between individuals and the larger community. Healthy, sound relationships are the fruit of mature, unselfish love.

> When the Son of Man comes in His glory, and all the angels with him, he will sit upon his throne, and all the nations will be assembled before him. And he will separate them one from another, as a shepherd separates the sheep from the goats. He will place the sheep on his right and the goats on his left. Then the king will say to those on his right, "Come, you who are blessed by my Father. Inherit the kingdom prepared for you from the foundation of the world. For I was hungry and you gave me food, I was thirsty and you gave me drink, a stranger and you welcomed me, naked and you clothed me, ill and you cared for me, in prison and you visited me." Then the righteous will answer

him and say, "Lord, when did we see you hungry and feed you, or thirsty and give you drink? When did we see you a stranger and welcome you, or naked and clothe you? When did we see you ill or in prison, and visit you?" And the king will say to them in reply, "Amen, I say to you, whatever you did for one of these least brothers of mine, you did for me." Then he will say to those on his left, "Depart from me, you accursed, into the eternal fire prepared for the devil and his angels. For I was hungry and you gave me no food, I was thirsty and you gave me no drink, a stranger and you gave me no welcome, naked and you gave me no clothing, ill and in prison, and you did not care for me." Then they will answer and say, "Lord, when did we see you hungry or thirsty or a stranger or naked or ill or in prison, and not minister to your needs." He will answer them, "Amen, I say to you, what you did not do for one of these least ones, you did not do for me." And these will go off to eternal punishment, but the righteous to eternal life.

Matthew 25:31-46

Love is the deepest reality and the deepest need of every human being, and it is the cornerstone of Jesus' teaching. For Jesus, the most important question, first and last, is, "Did you love?" The foundation of the Christian life is serving one another in love and even being willing to die so that others might live. To give our lives in the service of love does not mean that we lose our lives, and die, but that we find our lives more completely than ever through love.

Man was created in the image of God, and God is Love. This is why man is only truly human when he loves and becomes a reflection of God through his love. The more man loves, the more he becomes a reflection of God, and the closer he comes to all people and all creatures. It is very certain that man was not created simply to grow in the image of his family, or of his society, or even of his church. Before all else, man was created to grow in the image of his Creator, Who is Love.

Now we understand that the function of good families, good educators, and an effective parish is to help the individual grow in the image of God, and, as he does this, to make others happy and to become happy himself.

Now, to return to our original question. Who can measure the extent of our sin, or assess the extent of our virtue? The answer is quite simple. No one can personally measure the extent of sin because man did not determine sin in the first place. We can only expose those dangers which are poisoning and destroying love in our hearts, and these we have to root out completely.

Just as we have to root out the influences which are destroying love in our hearts, so too we have to nourish those resources which help us to become more loving. These resources are not just arbitrary inventions of the Church or some other educational institution. They are fundamental helps to man and without them he will not develop fully as he should. Specifically, the Christian is called to prayer, fasting, confession, participation at Mass, and the reading and meditation on Scripture. All of these will help the Christian to find his way to Christ and will nourish him on the way. Furthermore, Christians will take these resources seriously once they understand their responsibility to become spiritually mature.

11

Confession—Why?

Then he said, "A man had two sons, and the younger said to his father, 'Father, give me the share of your estate that should come to me.' So the father divided the property between them. After a few days, the younger son collected all his belongings and set off to a distant country where he squandered his inheritance on a life of dissipation. When he had freely spent everything, a severe famine struck that country, and he found himself in dire need. So he hired himself out to one of the local citizens who sent him to his farm to tend the swine. And he longed to eat his fill of the pods on which the swine fed, but nobody gave him any. Coming to his senses he thought, 'How many of my father's hired workers have more than enough food to eat, but here am I, dying from hunger. I shall get up and go to my father and I shall say to him, 'Father, I have sinned against heaven and against you. I no longer deserve to be called your son; treat me as you would treat one of your hired workers.' So he got up and went back to his father. While he was still a long way off, his father caught sight of him, and was filled with compassion. He ran to his son, embraced him and kissed him. His son said to him, 'Father, I have sinned against heaven and against you; I no longer deserve to be called your son.' But his father ordered his servants, 'Quickly bring the finest robe and put it on him; put a ring on his finger and sandals on his feet. Take the fattened calf and slaughter it. Then let us celebrate with a feast, because this son of mine was dead, and has come to life again, he was lost, and has been found.' Then the celebration began."

Luke 15:11-24

For many people, confession is an embarrassing moment when we reveal our sins, transgressions and imperfections to another person, and then wait to be reproached and reprimanded, and given a punishment. Often, confession involves accusing ourselves in front of a priest whom we don't even know, or it involves feeling shame as we accuse ourselves in front of a priest whom we do know. The most important sins we should confess may not be mentioned because we want to make a "good" impression on the priest.

Although both priests and believers acknowledge today that the sacrament of Confession is
going through a crisis, at the same time more
and more people are searching for someone to
talk with about their problems, their mental
anguish, their sins, and their wounds caused by
others. Many individuals, and sometimes even
whole families, are looking for psychiatrists and
counselors to give them advice and help them
to overcome their problems, and even to help
them with spiritual matters. Once they find some
responsible counselor, they open their heart and
soul, and invariably they are helped to overcome
their problems as they share with another person.
Human experience confirms that we are always
looking for another person to confide in, hoping
he or she will help to heal our heart and soul.
The more disorders we have in life, the more
wounds and suffering we have endured, the more
we need another person to listen to us, to help
calm and console us, and to bring us back to
peace.

In the sacrament of Confession we will find
just this kind of deep, trusting relationship. In
the sharing between the penitent and the priest,
one person listens in the strictest confidence to
the sins and problems of another. Even more
important, according to the will of Christ,
confession surpasses any other human meeting.
Because in confession the penitent meets with

God, his merciful Father, Who waits for him with joy and runs to embrace him, and give him a new robe, and welcomes him to the table of the community where all are sharing in God's joy and peace.

Therefore, in confession there is a real meeting between the human and the divine. This meeting is made possible through the deep sharing and trust between the penitent and the priest.

12

The Confessor

And all this is from God, Who has reconciled us to himself through Christ and given us the ministry of reconciliation, namely, God was reconciling the world to Himself in Christ, not counting their trespasses against them and entrusting to us the message of reconciliation. So we are ambassadors for Christ, as if God were appealing through us. We implore you on behalf of Christ, be reconciled to God. For our sake He made Him to be sin Who did not know sin, so that we might become the righteousness of God in Him.

2 Corinthians 5:19-21

The human ingredients in the sacrament of Confession, the meeting between the priest and the penitent, prepare the ground for divine action. Because of this, the role of the priest in confession is very important. We can readily compare the role of the priest in confession to the role of the doctor in the process of healing a patient. The doctor must understand disease and the symptoms of disease, and even more important, what medicine and therapy will heal the patient. It is the same with the priest. He must be a man of real faith, hope, and love, and also someone who is deeply knowledgeable about the spiritual life and the laws of spiritual growth. He must know how to listen in order to discern what is happening in the soul of the penitent. In this way, he fulfills his human role by making everything ready for God's divine action.

In his conversation with the penitent, he must encourage whatever seems right, caution wherever the penitent seems to be in danger, and sow the seeds of the divine word into the soul of the penitent.

Another name for the priest is the curator of souls. This means that he cares for our souls. He prepares our souls to be healed, and in the name of God, forgives the sins and heals the wounds of the penitent.

Along with his human knowledge and his understanding of the movements of the soul and heart, it is necessary for the priest, whenever possible, to know and to be acquainted with the penitent in order to understand and to guide him better. This means the penitent should introduce himself by saying who he is, what he does, as well as where he is from. He should give the priest some idea of his material, social and general moral background. He should also give a short history of his spiritual life. This is all very important, and enables the priest to give the penitent concrete advice and guidance, and help him to overcome his mistakes and move forward in acquiring virtue. This is why it is important for the penitent to return to the same confessor, and, if possible, for one priest to become his regular confessor. From time to time the penitent may go to another priest, but for a strong spiritual life, a regular confessor is important. A person without a strong spiritual life will shift confessors frequently, hoping to present himself favorably to a new priest. From a regular confessor he might fear questions regarding his failure to improve since his last confession. But confession is meant to be a friendly meeting between the one who seeks mercy, reconciliation, spiritual healing, and the absolution of his sins, and the one who listens to him in the name of God and says, "Do not be afraid. Your sins are pardoned. Go in peace and sin no more." When the confessor and the penitent meet in the sacrament of Confession they are celebrating God's mercy, God's love and God's forgiveness. Because of this, confession is always a celebration and a joyful meeting.

13

You Are Called to Confession

On March 25, 1985, the Feast of the Annunciation, Our Lady gave this message through Marija Pavlovic:

Dear Children! Today I wish to call you all to confession, even if you have confessed a few days ago. I wish that you all experience my feast day within yourselves. But you cannot experience it unless you abandon yourselves completely to God. Therefore, I am inviting you all to reconciliation with God!

This is one of the most striking messages in which Our Lady invites us to confession. Viewed in relation to the Feast of the Annunciation, one more thing about confession is clear.

Mary is the new Eve. She said, "Behold, I am

the handmaid of the Lord. May it be done unto me according to Thy word" (Luke 1:38). With these words of Mary, the handmaid of the Lord, a new world began.

The first woman, Eve, did not fulfill God's plan in her life. She sinned, and through sin man rejected God and His plans. Through sin, man preferred his own will, and rejected God's will. Mary brought healing to a world which was hurt by the disobedience of our first parents. It was possible because Christ, the new Adam, accepted the will of the Father and entered the world to save the world. He entered the world through Mary, the one who was the humble and obedient handmaid of the Lord.

Therefore, the deepest meaning of the Feast of the Annunciation stems not just from the fact that Christ, the Word Divine, became man for us by His Incarnation in the womb of the Virgin Mary, but even more, that through Mary's surrender to God's will a new history of salvation began.

From this great mystery and the reality of the Incarnation, which was dependent upon Mary's acceptance of the will of God, we discover the deep meaning of confession. Certainly it is no accident that Mary called us all to confession on her feast. This helps us to understand the question: What is confession?

Confession is the total and conscious acceptance of God's will and the renunciation of the world which enslaves and destroys us. It is the acceptance of God's salvation and light, peace, and love, and the renunciation of the world of darkness, hatred, and unrest.

Mary said, "You cannot experience a true celebration of this feast if you do not confess your sins." It means that you cannot begin a new life if you are not prepared to tell God, "Here I am, Lord, ready to do your will." It is God's will for us to seek forgiveness for all those areas where we oppose Him and prefer our will to His, and where we are really closer to the old Eve than we are to Mary, the new Eve. Therefore, confession is the moment when we can return to a life without sin and begin to build a new world. It is the moment when we allow God to enter our lives again, when we put Him first in our lives once more. It is also the moment when the old man in us is renewed by the power of Christ's Incarnation.

The more sincere we are in our confessions, and the more regularly we receive the sacrament, the closer we will come to celebrating the true spirit of the Annunciation which Mary, the Mother of all the living and the new Eve, refers to in her message. That celebration is a celebration of life, peace, joy, love, and true community between God and man, and men among themselves.

The closer we come to living what Mary is really leading us to in this message, the more we will renounce the destructive power of sin. We will become stronger when temptations arise, and we will have less fear and anxiety.

In this way we will enter into the glory of being children of God. This is why it is no accident that many pilgrims and priests in Medjugorje confirm that through the sacrament of Confession they have discovered the beauty and significance of the call to conversion, of returning to friendship between God and man.

Now the meaning of the ministry of reconciliation which has been given to priests becomes clearer in the eyes of both priests and believers. Surely, there is no ministry from one person to another more beautiful than the ministry of reconciliation.

14

Regarding Penance

Therefore, since we are surrounded by so great a cloud of witnesses, let us rid ourselves of every burden and sin that clings to us and persevere in running the race that lies before us while keeping our eyes fixed on Jesus, the Leader and Perfecter of faith. For the sake of the joy that lay before Him He endured the cross, despising its shame, and has taken His seat at the right of the throne of God. Consider how He endured such opposition from sinners, in order that you may not grow weary and lose heart. In your struggle against sin you have not yet resisted to the point of shedding blood. You have also forgotten the exhortation addressed to you as sons: My son, do not disdain the discipline of the Lord or lose heart when reproved by Him.

Hebrews 12:1-5

Usually the priest in confession assigns us something to do or asks us to pray some prayers; we call this penance. Recently, an adult who was inspired by the events in Medjugorje, decided to become a convert, and was preparing for the sacraments. After she made her first confession, the priest told her what prayers she was to recite for her penance. She was surprised by this, and in a perfectly serious tone repeated, "Penance? Didn't you tell me that it is a joy to be able to pray and to be called to prayer, and that the greatest joy is being able to say, 'I forgive,' and now in return I am forgiven? Because of that I will pray and it will not be penance for me, it will be joy."

Another person came to confession who had not been to the sacrament for years. At the end of sharing with the priest, he asked, "Please, Father, now tell me what my punishment is?" The priest answered, "There is no punishment, but as a sign of your good will and your promise to stop damaging and destroying yourself, please say the following prayers. . ."

What we call penance should not be understood as a punishment, or a denial of anything. Penance is a joyful part of confession, a concrete sign of our readiness to return to the One Who has called us to His table again. Just as conversion is a joyful act of deliverance from burdens and wounds, so penance is a sign of the act of confessing. Penance is a sign that God is giving us more time and a further opportunity for our life to grow and mature. Of itself, penance is a continuation of healing. The penance given might be something painful, but it is even better if it brings healing, and it should never produce a loss of hope. To have a correct understanding of penance means to be ready to fight constantly against sin and the ways we are offending ourselves, others, and God. For example, if someone drinks and disturbs peace in himself, his family, or his community, what could he be given for penance? Through prayer he should ask every day for the strength to resist the temptation to drink, until he is completely healed. For one who curses or who is always angry at others, what should be his penance? He should be asked to take special care of his soul every day until he changes its condition. If we have lost our consciousness of the meaning of penance, maybe something has happened which never should have happened. Maybe our understanding of sin, of its wounds and of our need for healing, has become superficial. Once this happens, we sometimes conclude that confession is of no benefit to us.

It is necessary that we cooperate with the grace that is given to us in the sacrament. If we don't cooperate, then everything is useless, just as it is useless to sow even the best seed on uncultivated or rocky ground.

Therefore, penance always includes an inner determination to guard the grace of healing and to work on our healing. Once we realize that it pays to be healthy, to be able to love, to forgive, to have mercy, then it will not be hard for us to take medicine for such a healing, even if we have to take it for the rest of our lives.

15

How to Prepare for Confession

> Now the works of the flesh are obvious:
> immorality, impurity, licentiousness, idolatry,
> sorcery, hatred, rivalry, jealousy, outbursts of
> fury, acts of selfishness, dissensions, factions,
> occasions of envy, drinking bouts, orgies, and
> the like. I warn you, as I warned you before,
> that those who do such things will not inherit
> the Kingdom of God.   Galatians 5:19-21

Anyone who wants to go to confession needs to prepare for the sacrament. This preparation is called an examination of conscience. The examination of conscience can be done many ways, but the goal is always the same, to see your life and your deeds and to examine them in front of God, in the light of God's truth, and according to the Word of Jesus Christ.

It is helpful to note two ways to examine ourselves. We can examine our conscience by recalling the sins we have committed, and then confess them. Or, we can examine ourselves before God and try to name the source, the root cause, of our sins.

Perhaps we will understand this better if we make a comparison to medicine. Often it is said that some doctors look only for the symptoms of sickness and then immediately give medicine. But there is another approach which looks not so much for the symptoms of sickness as for the root causes of the sickness which are producing the symptoms. For example, someone can have a headache and take medicine to cure it, without knowing that the cause of the headache might be from nervousness or other things.

It is the same with confession. We can say that we were angry, but we should also be able to say why we were angry. If our work is not going well, and we are acting selfishly and proudly and irritated with others, perhaps it is because they are not conforming to our wishes. In other words, as we prepare carefully for confession, we need to talk more about the root causes of our sins, even more than about the sins themselves. For example, someone can confess that he does not pray. But, the real problem might be deep within himself, in his lack of faith or in his failure to depend on God. Therefore, when he confesses that he does not pray, he should acknowledge that his faith has grown lukewarm and that he is no longer committed to real spiritual growth. Once we learn to examine our deepest interior attitudes, then we will begin to make real progress.

We must always be prepared to ask ourselves, "Am I doing everything I can to grow in faith, hope, and love?" Even though specific sins motivate us to examine our conscience, the most important reason for the examination is to deepen our faith and love. We do not examine ourselves simply to expose our sins, but to find the best way in which to mature as Christians.

Our preparation for confession should also be done in the light of the Ten Commandments of God. They will help us to create a correct relationship with God, with man, with ourselves, and with all things.

Finally, when Jesus commanded us to love God above all things and to love our neighbor as ourselves, He was giving us the whole measure for the examination of our lives. These two commandments contain the whole law and the prophets.

The standard of the two great commandments is the only measure by which Jesus is going to recognize his own, and reward them or reject them. We can examine our lives most fruitfully under the light of these two commandments, for they provide the easiest way to see our own omissions and the omissions of others. By examining our life against them, we discover how firm our own Christian life and efforts are.

16

Contrition

In order to make a good confession, contrition is necessary. Contrition means that we are truly sorry for our sins, because we have not tried harder to grow in love, and because through sin, we have damaged ourselves and our gifts. Certainly, contrition also includes a firm decision to fight against any sin that is destroying us, and a determination to use every possible resource to help ourselves grow in love. Only after we have really grasped how serious not growing in holiness is and how we destroy ourselves by sin, can we say genuinely from our hearts, "I am sorry and I will never do that again."

Sometimes we are unsure of ourselves and we say, "I am sorry, but I cannot promise that this will not happen again. If I know that this will happen to me again, then my confession is insincere, and I am a liar in front of myself and

God." The truth is, that because of our weaknesses and the way the world is, it is very difficult to achieve a state in which we do everything according to the command of love toward God and our neighbor.

It is not good to become tense and fearful by thinking this way. Rather we should trust that with God's help and God's mercy, we will move forward in life. Each day, we should direct all our efforts to become more perfect, and through love, to grow closer to God and to our neighbor. Then we will begin to realize how much our self destruction offends and "saddens" God.

The availability of confession and the call for monthly confession help us to understand that we can be genuinely contrite without being perfect. But, we must go to confession and return from confession with a firm conviction to do everything possible to grow in love and to avoid all sin and all evil. Once we begin living our lives with total determination and this kind of conviction we will succeed more easily. Therefore, it is very important to create in our own hearts a real desire for growth, and a decision to foster it. Contrition definitely presumes a decision to avoid all the places and occasions which make us fall easily into sin. Frequent confession protects and fosters this decision.

17

The Action of Satan

In our discussion of sin and the healing of sin through the sacrament of Reconciliation, it is important and helpful to remember the obvious in the messages of Our Lady in Medjugorje. Our Lady often stresses, simply and clearly, that Satan exists. He is active and wants to bring unrest, to stir up hatred and to spread evil. She reminds us that we should not cooperate with him. She tells us not to fear Satan, but to pray and to love, and then everything will be turned to good.

The truth is that we have all discovered evil and evil habits within ourselves which lead us to destruction and to sin. When we are attracted to evil in this way, we are not alone. There is something outside of us which is urging us to do evil, in the same way that the world cooperates with Evil. Even more, Satan can directly influence our decisions, prompting us to certain pleasures, averting us from doing good, and advising us to do evil. For example, many men, when they are praying, have experienced intense thoughts of cursing or a desire to insult the sacred, and so on. Some people are frightened by these thoughts, and they feel guilty. That is not right. People with these tendencies should not condemn themselves. Whenever this happens, the person tempted should quietly continue praying and blessing God. Such a response can benefit the individual as well as others bothered by the same problem, because now, there is someone redeeming the curser and other contrite sinners. On the one hand, it is not necessary to look everywhere for Satan and blame everything on him. When we do, we can cooperate with him. We can cooperate freely with evil through our decisions and with our evil habits. On the other hand, we should not completely exclude the influence of Satan. It is certain that he will not let anyone go completely undisturbed, especially not the one who has decided to glorify the name of God, the person who will not curse; especially not the one who has decided to love and to forgive and to stop hating; especially not the one who has decided to stop drinking and to be careful on every possible occasion; especially not the one who has decided to stop misusing the gift of sexuality and who begins to conform to God's desires. Satan is not naive. He knows who is an obstacle for him. He knows whom he should tempt, whom he should discourage, and whom he should lead into evil.

In confession, it is helpful for the priest to ask the penitent if there is any power which is especially urging or forcing him to commit sin. If the temptation is to evil and to something destructive, then without exaggeration it can be said that it is a work of Satan.

Devout souls who desire to serve God totally will be especially tempted in this way.

> Be sober and vigilant. Your opponent the devil is prowling around like a roaring lion looking for someone to devour. Resist him, steadfast in faith, knowing that your fellow believers throughout the world undergo the same sufferings. The God of all grace Who called you to His eternal glory through Christ Jesus will himself restore, confirm, strengthen, and establish you after you have suffered a little. To him, be dominion forever. Amen.
>
> I Peter 5:8-11

Dear Children! I beseech you to take up the way of holiness beginning today. I love you, and, therefore, I want you to be holy. I do not want Satan to block you on that way. Dear children, pray and accept all that God is offering you on a way which is bitter. But at the same time, God will reveal every sweetness to whomever begins to go on that way, and he will gladly answer every call of God. Do not attribute importance to petty things. Long for heaven. Thank you for having responded to my call.

July 25, 1987

Dear Children! These days Satan wants to frustrate my plans. Pray that his plan will not be realized. I will pray to my Son Jesus to give you the grace to experience the victory of Jesus in the temptations of Satan. Thank you for having responded to my call.

July 12, 1984

We should guard ourselves against Satan not only to protect our own salvation but also to protect the salvation of the whole world. For this reason Our Lady urges us to fight against Satan:

Dear Children! Today I call you especially now to advance against Satan by means of prayer. Satan wants to work still more now that you know he is at work. Dear children, put on the armor for battle and with the rosary in your hand defeat him! Thank you for having responded to my call.

August 8, 1985

18

Preparation for Confession

Examination of Conscience with Thanksgiving

There are many different ways to examine our conscience. The foundation for every examination of conscience is the review of our relationship with God, our neighbor, ourselves and all creatures. Let us now examine our conscience and use the theme of thanksgiving as the framework for our questions and answers, prayers, and meditations.

To do this better, we need to understand what thanksgiving is. Thanksgiving is a synonym for faith. Whoever is thankful to God truly recognizes God as his Master and Creator. He accepts God in his life. To be thankful also means to accept joyfully the gifts which God gives us and then to use them according to His will.

To be thankful means to believe with our hearts, and to believe with our hearts means to acknowledge God continually, to discover Him in everything, and always to cooperate with Him.

Thankfulness means not only that we say "Thank You" to God, but that we also cooperate with Him. This cooperation is what it means when we say in the Our Father, "Thy will be done." Using this idea of thankfulness, we should examine ourselves before God, other people, ourselves, the whole created world and all creatures.

We are guilty of ingratitude when we deny God and His gifts, when we refuse to cooperate with God or with others, and finally, when we misuse our gifts.

The seed of a flower demonstrates thankfulness or gratitude when it grows and with its beauty makes the world more beautiful. If all the seeds in the world refused to develop and destroyed their own growth and maturation, we would never again have flowers, or fruit. All life would eventually be destroyed. Man expresses his most profound gratitude when he allows God to work in him. As each individual grows and matures, God is glorified. Man's most profound ingratitude is shown when he refuses to cooperate with God and only half develops his potential.

Those who are familiar with Mary's Medjugorje messages know that every message ends with thanksgiving. Our Lady always says, "Thank you for having responded to my call." Our Lady not only expresses her thankfulness in every message, but she devotes some messages entirely to calling us to thanksgiving:

Dear Children! Today I invite you to give thanks to God for all the gifts that you have discovered in the course of your life, and even for the least gift that you have received. I give thanks with you and want all of you to experience the joy of these gifts; and I want God to be everything for each one of you. And then, little children, you can grow continuously on the way of holiness. Thank you for having responded to my call.
September 25, 1989

Thankfulness to God

And be thankful. Let the word of Christ dwell in you richly, as in all wisdom you teach and admonish one another, singing psalms, hymns, and spiritual songs with gratitude in your hearts to God. And whatever you do, in word or in deed, do everything in the name of the Lord Jesus, giving thanks to God the Father through him.

Colossians 3:15-17

Prayer

O God, my Creator, I confess that You are my God. I choose You for my Lord. Thank You for being my Lord and for creating me. All glory and praise to You, because You called me into life from the deepest nothingness. Thank You that I can return to You now just as the prodigal son returned to his father.

Your fatherly heart is full of mercy and forgiveness. Thank You for rejoicing that I am returning to You.

Father, I want to come before You, and to be with You, and I know that You want to be with me. Just as Your heart once grieved when I drifted far from You and I became a lonely foreigner living my life without You, now Your heart rejoices because I am returning to You, filled with thankfulness.

Here I am, Father. Send me Your Holy Spirit to teach me how to find You. May Your Spirit enlighten me. May this reunion with You bring me unending joy, because You are going to renew me. I will praise Your goodness and mercy, and I will proclaim Your faithfulness.

Father, I am deeply sorry that I have not always had You first in my life.

I was deceived when I allowed material things and creatures to dominate my feelings and thoughts. I offended You, just as a child offends and disappoints his parents when he forgets them and turns to other people, to material pleasures and distractions, thinking that in them he will find salvation and peace.

I am sorry for wanting to be powerful like You, and for deciding what is good and bad for me without ever asking for Your help. I am sorry that I have often relied entirely on myself, convinced that I knew better than you did what was right and wrong. By doing this, I have led myself and others into many errors. So many times, Lord, I have resisted Your holy will.

I am sorry because I have often been overcome with fear and mistrust. In this way, I have tortured and deceived myself, forgetting that it is not necessary to worry and to be fearful. You take care of everyone in life who seeks Your Kingdom and its justice. With my behavior towards You, I have lost the dignity You gave me through baptism. I am sorry.

You have empowered me to draw close to You in prayer, in the Mass, in confession and in Communion. Often I have been careless toward You and I have neglected these opportunities to be with You, and in this way, I have rejected Your help.

Thank You, for giving me freedom when You created me. Forgive me for using my freedom to decide against Your holy will. You have always wanted what is best for me and best for others.

With this confession, Father, I want to decide totally for You. I give You my wounded heart, my heart that has been broken by sin, my heart that is not filled with goodness, love, peace and joy, as it should be. Please, forgive me, and renew me through this confession.

Please, fill my confessor with Your merciful love. In Your name, he is now going to restore my life and to help me find You again. Lord, help him to belong to You. May his heart choose You in all things. May he be able to renounce all other masters. May he be delivered from every addiction. May You be everything to him, so that as Your servant, he can teach me and encourage me in Your name. Open his heart and ears, so that he will be able to understand me and lead me correctly.

Forgive me, because I have failed to love You as my Lord and Savior in all people and in all creatures. Lord, I pray for everyone who has ever known You and has ever belonged to You, but has strayed from you. May Your fatherly heart rejoice whenever they return to You. I pray, too, for those who have never heard about You or known You.

I pray for all parents who have not taught their children to put You first in their lives. Forgive them, and show them that You are Lord and Savior of all. Also, please, look mercifully on those who consciously work against You. They are also Your children. In the name of all those who refuse to acknowledge You, I renounce the sin of atheism. I ask You, please, to reveal Your love to the whole world so that everyone will accept You and serve You, the way Mary served You, and the way Your son Jesus served You.

> My soul proclaims the greatness of the Lord; my spirit rejoices in God my savior. For he has looked upon His handmaid's lowliness; behold, from now on will all ages call me blessed. The Mighty One has done great things for me, and holy is His name. His mercy is from age to age to those who fear Him. He has shown might with His arm, dispersed the arrogant of mind and heart. He has thrown down the rulers from their thrones but lifted up the lowly. The hungry He has filled with good things; the rich He has sent away empty. He has helped Israel His servant remembering His mercy, according to His promise to our fathers, to Abraham and to his descendants forever.

Luke 1:46-56

(Remain in silence and examine your conscience, so that you can correct your relationship with God and grow as He desires.)

Dear children! Today also I am inviting you to prayer. I am always inviting you, but you are still far away. Therefore, from today, decide seriously to dedicate time to God. I am with you and I desire to teach you to pray with the heart. In prayer with the heart you shall encounter God. Therefore, little children, pray, pray, pray. Thank you for having responded to my call.
October 25, 1989

Thank You for the Gift of Life

So I declare and testify in the Lord that you must no longer live as the Gentiles do, in the futility of their minds; darkened in understanding, alienated from the life of God because of their ignorance, because of their hardness of heart, they have become callous and have handed themselves over to licentiousness for the practice of every kind of impurity to excess. That is not how you learned Christ, assuming that you have heard of Him and were taught in Him, as truth is in Jesus, that you should put away the old self of your former way of life, corrupted through deceitful desires, and be renewed in the spirit of your minds, and put on the new self, created in God's way in righteousness and holiness of truth.

Ephesians 4:17-24

Prayer

Lord, Creator of all things, thank You for creating life. I praise and glorify You because You have called me into existence out of nothing. Today, I consciously accept the gift of my life. You created me in the womb of my mother. Blessed are You for Your power of creation. Bless my father and my mother. Thank You for their love through which they accepted me and took care of me. Thank You that I too am able to love. Thank You for wanting to enrich my life with Your love.

Heavenly Father, I have to confess that I have not always accepted responsibility for the life You gave me. I confess that I have damaged my life through sin.

Often, I have allowed pride and selfishness to choke the gift of love in me or to prevent the growth of real love. I also have damaged my life by not devoting enough time to my spiritual growth and the growth of my soul. I have sinned against my life by paying more attention to the needs of my body than to my soul's need to grow in faith, hope, love, patience, humility, and faithfulness.

I realize that I have damaged my friendship with You because I did not develop the gifts You gave me. I was lazy, and ignored many graces You sent me. I rejected many opportunities You gave me to grow in goodness. I allowed myself to remain undeveloped, incomplete and immature. You wanted me to become mature. You wanted to be proud of me just as every father is proud of his child who grows up to resemble his mother and father. By neglecting my body and my spirit, I have remained an incomplete person, an imperfect reflection of my own world. Because I have stopped growing, I have not been an effective witness of Your love, Your mercy and Your forgiveness. Forgive me.

I am sorry that I have misused my freedom, my gift of speech, my work, and my ability to cooperate with You. Forgive me because I have allowed material things to enslave me, and often my preoccupation with them has damaged my relationship with You and with others.

I have often been agitated and angry. I have disagreed with others and have not tried to understand them.

Forgive me, because I have neglected Your

graces, and by doing so I have damaged myself immensely. Today, I once more accept my life with gratitude. I want to cooperate gratefully with Your holy will. Until now, because of my carelessness, I have become nothing more than a fruitless fig tree. Today, I am deciding to cooperate with You with my whole heart.

Thank You for Your forgiveness, for allowing me to begin again and to hope for new growth.

Thank You, because in me the expression, "O happy sin," comes to life when I receive Your love and Your mercy.

Send me Your Spirit. May He lead me. May He open me to the fullness of life that You want to give me.

(Remain in silence and examine specific areas of sin in your life. Maybe you have been destroying yourself with alcohol or drugs, by eating too much, or working too much, thus creating an imbalance between your body and soul. Maybe these disorders entered your life through destructive and immoral sexual behavior, by which you have damaged the maturity of your senses. In misusing this gift maybe you have become an egoist, a self-centered person thinking only about your own enjoyment. . .)

Heavenly Father, through this confession now,

please heal me, and enable me to cooperate totally with You. From this moment onwards, may my life glorify You, and benefit all those around me. I do not want to remain an immature plant in Your garden, nor do I want to be a fruitless fig tree in Your orchard. I especially do not want to be a source of destruction in Your kingdom.

I want to be like the city built on top of the mountain, or like the lighted lamp that is put on the lampstand, and help others to find the way.

I want to be like the mustard seed which unfolds and grows even though, of itself, it is so small. I want You to be able to use me as a mature and reliable servant in Your kingdom. Thank You for not turning Your face away from me. Thank You for granting me another opportunity.

Cleanse my heart from the wounds of sin and evil within me, and from all my negative feelings. I want to grow and to bear fruit which will prove that I am living according to Your Spirit.

May this meeting with You become a fountain of life within me. May everything within me bloom again and bring forth fruit. May my renewal be like spring rain falling on dry land, or like the spring sun shining on frozen ground. Just as a mother's tenderness brings the best out of her child, so God's love restores His followers. May the power of Your Spirit heal my disorders, and restore my original peace, which I lost when sin controlled me.

Inspire me now to walk anew with You. Help me to understand that my Christian life involves more than just guarding myself from sin. It also involves committing myself to growing in holiness and goodness, just as You, Father desire for me.

Father, I pray now for the priest to whom I will be going to confession. Help him to become the kind of priest You want him to be. May his love, faith, hope, joy, peace, patience, goodness, wisdom and fortitude inspire me to renounce all my personal sins. May I always cooperate with You. Bless my confessor and enable him to fulfill his human and priestly vocation. Fill my confessor with Your Spirit so that, in Your name, he will give me good advice. May he find the right words to inspire me and help me to grow and to become more and more like You. Give him strength and wisdom to recognize and to help me see everything that is not in order in my life. From now on may my life bring You glory and praise. Amen.

Thank You for My Neighbor

Therefore, putting away falsehood, speak the truth, each one to his neighbor, for we are members one of another. Be angry but do not sin; do not let the sun set on your anger, and do not leave room for the devil. The thief must no longer steal, but rather labor, doing honest work with his own hands, so that he may have something to share with one in need. No foul language should come out of your mouths, but only such as is good for needed edification, that it may impart grace to those who hear. And do not grieve the Holy Spirit of God, with which you were sealed for the day of redemption. All bitterness, fury, anger, shouting, and reviling must be removed from you, along with all malice. And be kind to one another, compassionate, forgiving one another as God has forgiven you in Christ.

Ephesians 4:25-32

Prayer

Dear God, You used other persons to create me and to raise me. Now I consciously thank You for all the people around me. You gifted them to help me lead a fully human life, and through them You have taught me and have led me.

Forgive me, because I have often misunderstood others. I have offended them, hurt them, neglected them, despised them, ignored them, calumniated them, spoken ill of them, and have been impatient, impolite, and unfaithful to them. I understand what it means to sin against my neighbor. It means that I can hurt my neighbor, confuse him, damage him, or discourage him. I can block the light on his path and stop his growth in love. I can also destroy his peace.

I understand why Jesus said, "Love your neighbor as yourself." My neighbor is meant to be a gift to me. He is not meant to annoy me, to anger me, or to incite me to evil. Rather, by his presence and his giftedness, he is meant to help me grow. How often have I been ungrateful towards others, when all my life depends on them? I am especially sorry for failing to love my parents more, because they gave me life. They have cared for me so generously, and they have done everything for me. I am sorry for failing to love them during the times they were unable to love me. When they argued with each other, or rejected one another, or humiliated and abandoned one another, then I condemned them. I did not try to understand them and their difficulties. Forgive me, my God.

Forgive me, because there were many people who came into my life who had been rejected, and despised, and who quarreled with others. They were forsaken, poor and persecuted. My indifference to them is a sign to me now that my love for my neighbor was not perfect. Forgive me for the times when I forget that the sacred flame of love dwells in each person. Often I was too preoccupied with unimportant things, making poor use of the opportunities and the gifts that You gave me.

Forgive me for the indifference I showed toward others when I was preoccupied with my own personal problems.

Forgive me for refusing to listen to others, and insisting on my own way. I resented them and would not allow them to develop their gifts.

I understand now that every disorder in my life and in my behavior is sinful because it prevents others from growing and causes them to sin, even those whom You send to support me.

I am also sorry for every sin in my affections and in my sexuality. You gave me my sexuality. You created the attraction between the sexes. It is Your will that husbands and wives complete each other and become one body and one spirit.

You know, O God, how many times I have misused my sexuality when, in selfishness, I turned to myself and sought self-satisfaction, thinking only of pleasing myself. I realize that with this sin I have damaged my maturity and have not exercised self-control.

You also know, Lord, that I have used others, and they have used me. Many times I have been scandalized because others acted as if they were not fully human and used their sexuality in a degrading way. Forgive me, and help me to use my sexuality as You have ordained it to be used.

(Now examine yourself honestly and then talk with the priest sincerely. Do this especially if you have difficulties with your sexuality, or find yourself in difficult circumstances, or if you have unusual disorders. It is not that the priest is curious about these things, but that the sacrament of Confession will help you come to real order in your sexuality.)

I pray for all those with whom I have sinned, and for all those I have led into some disorder. I pray for those who are suffering because of disorder in their sexual life.

Forgive us, Lord, for in this world we often misuse the gift of sexuality, and disgrace the temple of our body which You built with Your powers of creation.

Lord, I want to offer You all victims of sexual abuse. I seek Your mercy for all those who have raped others, seduced children, or desecrated the sacredness of their own bodies.

I pray for the conversion of those who have despised natural family planning in their marriages, or have gone outside their marriages to satisfy their passions, and thus have become slaves of their passions.

Have mercy on all homosexuals and lesbians. Save those who have sold themselves in prostitution. Wake up and convert all who own houses of prostitution, and who devote their lives to seducing others.

In this world, these sins are all common. They cause us much suffering. Forgive the whole world, Lord, and have mercy on us.

I pray for all those who are sick and have AIDS. I also pray for those who, through weakness or seductive powers, have misused their sexuality.

Forgive us for every abuse of this gift, so that we can be healed and truly learn to love one another.

Lord, many of us suffer greatly because we are nervous and impatient. We are too attached to material things and people. We often destroy ourselves and trample other persons and things.

Lord, cleanse us and our relationships, so that our love toward our neighbor may become perfect.

(Remain in silence and examine your attitude towards your neighbor. Ask if there is pride in you that you have been ignoring. Is there anything else in your heart which might extinguish the sacred flame of love within you towards others?)

Holy Father, make me willing to love You in my neighbors. I seek forgiveness from You now for the ways I have destroyed Your gifts in others and in myself. Lord, give us all the strength to forgive one another. May we be united and help one another to grow in holiness and gratitude for all that Your love is calling us to do and is enabling us to accomplish.

Give others the strength to forgive me, and help me to accept their forgiveness. Now, I am deciding again for the sacred flame of love which burns within me and within every man. I will do everything to protect this flame and keep it burning. May it constantly inspire my heart and the hearts of my neighbors.

Mary, Mother of all of us, through your intercession may we all become your sons and daughters. Help us grow in love towards one another.

May our peace and love for one another be signs that we belong to you. Under your protection, may the sacred flame of love increase and become stronger in every family, in every community, in the Church and in the world. Virgin and Mother, in whom virginity and motherhood are joined, help us protect the sacred flame and never let it be extinguished. And, if it does go out, may we turn to the Originator of the divine flame once more, and may we never again remain in darkness. Amen.

Thank You for All Creation

But a shoot shall sprout from the stump of Jesse, and from his roots a bud shall blossom. The spirit of the Lord shall rest upon him: a spirit of wisdom and of understanding, a spirit of counsel and of strength, knowledge and of fear of the Lord, and his delight shall be the fear of the Lord. Not by appearance shall he judge, nor by hearsay shall he decide, But he shall judge the poor with justice, and decide aright for the land's afflicted. He shall strike the ruthless with the rod of his mouth, and with the breath of his lips he shall slay the wicked. Justice shall be the band around his waist, and faithfulness a belt upon his hips.

Then the wolf shall be a guest of the lamb,

and the leopard shall lie down with the kid;
The calf and the young lion shall browse
together, with a little child to guide them. The
cow and the bear shall be neighbors, together
their young shall rest; the lion shall eat hay
like the ox. The baby shall play by the cobra's
den, and the child lay his hand on the adder's
lair. There shall be no harm or ruin on all
my holy mountain; for the earth shall be filled
with knowledge of the Lord, as water covers
the sea.

Isaiah 11:1-10

Prayer

Father, in heaven, You created the earth and
everything on it, and You entrusted its care to
man. You wanted us to cultivate the earth by
working and using the gifts which we have
received from You.

Today I confess to You my sin. I have misused
Your creatures and often disregarded Your Laws.
I have often denied You as Lord of my life, and
allowed creatures to enslave me by serving them
before serving You. Very frequently, I have
focused more on owning and enjoying things than
I have on serving You. Because of my bondage
to material objects, I have resisted Your will and
ended up in conflicts with the people around me.
I have envied others who had more than I had
or knew more than I knew. My preoccupation

with material things absorbed me, and I often forget that You alone are my supreme good. Forgive me.

Today, before going to confession, I want to decide once and for all to make You Lord of my life. I renounce all slavery to material objects. My absorption in them has caused me to quarrel, to fight, to hate, to envy and to be jealous. You alone are my God. May I never turn back on this decision.

I have often been selfish and possessive towards the gifts You entrusted to me. I ignored those who had less than I had and I focused only on those who had more than I had, and I envied them. When You gave me material gifts, You wanted me to be satisfied with them, and then to share them with others. Forgive me. I have not done this. Forgive me, because I took for granted all that I had. I stopped acknowledging that all my gifts were from You, and I focused only on what I didn't have. Then, I spent my days rushing to accumulate more things. From now on, I want nothing more than to manage well what You have given me.

Give me the grace to know how to praise You, because You have wonderfully given me all that I need. Forgive me. I have often overlooked this.

Father, there is something else I must confess to You. I have misused many of the gifts which have come to me from nature. I have damaged my life by indulging excessively in food and drink. You do not want me to do this because You know how harmful it is for me.

(Here, those who are damaging themselves with excessive consumption of food and drink should examine themselves carefully. Also, those who are misusing drugs or other things which are destroying their human potential and keeping them from maturing in love, and which are hurting the people around them, should examine themselves carefully.)

Father, You formed the earth to produce many different fruits, but we have turned the fruits of the earth against ourselves and against others. For example, You created iron so that we could make worthwhile and useful things with it, but we have forged much of it into weapons. Now, we are destroying ourselves and conducting wars against one another. In the name of all mankind, I ask forgiveness for all the ways we have misused Your creation. Forgive us for the wars we have started. Heal all our wounds.

Help us to use all of creation responsibly and with love, and to reestablish the original order which You intended should reign between man and nature.

Forgive all of us, for we are all guilty of destroying one another and endangering the life of our whole species.

Forgive us, because nature herself is suffering from our abuses. Make us determined to remedy everything. Help us not to allow any more suffering to come to creatures, as Saint Paul cautions us. Father, I have examined how I stand before You, before myself, before my neighbor and before all creatures. I come to You now, aware of the great trust You have placed in me. I admit that I have abused Your trust. I come seeking Your forgiveness and Your merciful love. I pray, please do not condemn me as You condemned the fruitless fig tree.

Give me the grace to cooperate with You in everything from now on. I am sincerely sorry for all the disorders through which I have destroyed myself and others. I am deeply sorry for ignoring You and misusing Your gifts. Touch my heart with the power of Your Spirit. I pray that deep within my soul every commitment and desire which comes from evil will change.

Father, in this confession renew me completely, so that I may glorify Your love, Your mercy and Your forgiveness.

Mary, the new Eve and Mother of all, teach

me to accept the will of the Father, and call me to confess my sins. Be with me now. Mary, please obtain grace for me, so that from now on I will always be able to say simply and humbly, "Here I am Lord. I am ready to do Your will." Mary, teach me not to resist God's will any more. Show me how to do God's will in every moment, when it is easy or difficult. Help me to be victorious over my sins and over the sins of the whole world. By your humility, Mary, you overcame evil and became coredemptorix with Jesus. Help me, so that my life will contribute to the glory of the heavenly Father here on earth.

Mother of the living, be with me. Amen.

19

A Prayer for
the Priest Confessor

The spirit of the Lord God is upon me, because
the Lord has anointed me;
He has sent me to bring glad tidings to the
lowly, to heal the broken hearted,
To proclaim liberty to the captives and release
to the prisoners,
To announce a year of favor from the Lord
and a day of vindication by our God,
To comfort all who mourn;
To place on those who mourn in Zion a
diadem instead of ashes,
To give them oil of gladness in place of
mourning, a glorious mantle instead of a
listless spirit.
They will be called oaks of justice, planted
by the Lord to show his glory.

Isaiah 61:1-3

Prayer

Thank You, Father in heaven, for sending Your Son, Jesus Christ, as the great Priest, to accomplish our salvation. Thank You, for He is our **peace.** He came to destroy hatred, sin and death. I bless You and praise You, because You gave Your apostles the power to pardon sin in Your name, and to heal wounded hearts with the power of Your mercy. Thank You for the ministry of reconciliation which You entrusted to Your Church. Be blessed and praised, O my Lord, because You have called me to the priesthood, and entrusted me with the ministry of reconciliation through the Church.

Thank You, because now, through me, You want to pour out Your merciful love on all Your children, on all Your sons and daughters who are wounded or who have lost the way.

Jesus, thank You, for by Your blood You have redeemed the world and reconciled the world to the Father. Thank You for Your gentle and humble heart. Thank You for Your goodness and mercy. Jesus, the Great Priest, I ask You now to heal my heart of every evil. Heal every wound still in my soul, so that in Your name, I can lovingly receive every human heart wounded by sin. Grant me the grace of reconciliation, so that in Your name I can always say, "Go in peace. Your sins are forgiven."

Lord Jesus, I pray to You for every person who will come to me for reconciliation. Bless every wounded heart who will open itself to me because of their trust in You. Enable me to listen with Your love. Through Your mercy, let me restore their hope.

I pray for those who are afraid and who, because of their fear, have been insincere in previous confessions and thus burdened themselves even more. Make my heart sensitive to them. Never let words of condemnation appear on my lips, but only merciful words which will redeem with the power of Your name. Pour out Your Holy Spirit on every soul who is seeking the sacrament of Confession. Heal every heart wounded by sin. Grant, to all those who confess, the power to grow continually in love and peace from now on. Fill the heart of everyone who confesses their sins and who seeks forgiveness with the fullness of Your gifts. May everyone who is renewed and healed by the power of this sacrament overcome all temptations and trials. Grant them the strength to resist whatever destroys them and to preserve the sacred flame which You have kindled in their hearts once more by the power of this sacrament.

Look mercifully on those who are locked in sin, and are addicted to material things. Grant them the freedom which only You can give.

Give a new strength and courage to those who are disappointed with themselves because they fall into sin again and again. Help them not to despair in their fight against sin. Make me sensitive to every problem, so that I can administer Your salvation. Bless every person's decision to repent. By the power of Your Spirit enlighten those who do not realize how sin is destroying them. May they receive the grace to decide firmly to resist evil. May everyone come to confession with the resolve of the prodigal son, "I will turn back and return to my Father."

Mary, my Mother, and Mother of Christ the Lord, the Great Priest, Mother of all who come to confession, I consecrate myself to you. Receive me as you received your Son Jesus. Help me to listen to your children and to encourage them with your love.

I recommend to you Mary, my Mother, all who will come to confession. They are yours. You have invited them through your motherly love. Mother of goodness, love, mercy and peace, help them to grow in goodness, love, mercy and peace. I place all of them under your pro tection. Under the mantle of your motherly protection, may they receive the strength to resist evil and sin. May they crush the head of Satan, and may they overcome all his seductions. As Mother, please encourage those who are afraid. Bind up the wounds of those who are hurt. Teach those who do not understand that every confession is a celebration of God's love. Enable every penitent to rejoice and to say with you, "My soul proclaims the greatness of the Lord, for He has done great things for me," through Christ, Our Lord. Amen.

20

Approaching the Priest

Father, bless me, so that I will make this holy confession according to the will of God and according to the teaching of the holy Church.

—My last confession was. . . *(say approximately how long.)*

—Confess your sins and ask for advice. Listen to the priest and what he has to say and remember whatever he tells you to do for penance.

(If you do not know the act of contrition, at the end you can pray this way.)

Prayer
Father in heaven, I am sorry for all the evil I have done. I am sorry that I have resisted Your will with my sins, and I have hurt myself and others. I have been ungrateful to You.

I renounce Satan and all his deeds. I renounce all evil. I promise that I will constantly strive to grow in love through the power of Your Spirit.

Thank You, Father, because You renew me and enable me to do good again. Grant me the grace to avoid every evil with all my heart, and to defend always what is right.

I am sorry that I have rejected Your love and Your goodness, and that I have cast myself out from Your banquet. Bless me and heal me. Amen.

21

After Confession

Prayer
Father, in heaven, thank You for having renewed me in this confession through Jesus Christ. Thank You for the joy and peace that I feel now. Thank You for the decisions I have made. Thank You because now I can return to Your table which You prepared for me with Your love. Feed my hunger and quench my thirst. Fill me with Your love. Enlighten me where I have fallen into darkness. Put me back on the right path where I was lost. Enable me to live joyfully with You from now on.

I pray for all those who are searching for Your love, but do not have the strength to come to Your table. May they all be reconciled to You and return joyously to Your banquet table of love.

I pray for all those who do not have the strength

to resist evil. Convert them and invite them to sit down at Your table. Let no one be excluded from the final feast which You have prepared for Your sons and daughters, through Jesus Christ.

I give You my wounded heart again, and all the wounded hearts throughout the world. Please renew them. From this moment onwards, enable us to be grateful to You, and enable us to use all the gifts You have given us in the way you intended them to be used. May this be accomplished now and forever, for me and for all people everywhere. Amen.

Supplement to the Examination of Conscience

I

For Those Who Insult or Curse Your Holy Name, Lord

(for those who curse)

Not many of you should become teachers, my brothers, for you realize that we will be judged more strictly, for we all fall short in many respects. If anyone does not fall short in speech, he is a perfect man, able to bridle his whole body also. If we put bits into the mouths of horses to make them obey us, we also guide their whole bodies. It is the same with ships: even though they are so large and driven by fierce winds, they are steered by a very small rudder wherever the pilot's inclination wishes. In the same way the tongue is a small member and yet has great pretensions.

Consider how a small fire can set a huge
forest ablaze. The tongue is also a fire. It exists
among our members as a world of malice,
defiling the whole body and setting the entire
course of our lives on fire, itself set on fire
by Gehenna. For every kind of beast and bird,
of reptile and sea creature, can be tamed and
has been tamed by the human species, but no
human being can tame the tongue. It is a
restless evil, full of deadly poison. With it we
bless the Lord and Father, and with it we curse
human beings who are made in the likeness
of God. From the same mouth come blessing
and cursing. This need not be so, my brothers.
Does a spring gush forth from the same
opening both pure and brackish water? Can
a fig tree, my brothers, produce olives, or a
grapevine figs? Neither can salt water yield
fresh.

James 3:1-12

Father, may Your Holy Name be praised and
glorified. Thank You, because You have revealed
to Your children the holiness of Your Name.
Millions of Your children throughout the world
pray every day, "Hallowed by Thy name." May
You be praised, glorified and blessed through Your
Son Jesus Christ, Who glorified the holiness of
Your name and taught us to revere Your name.
May You be praised, glorified and blessed in the
Blessed Virgin Mary, the Mother of Your Son, and

Mother of us all. She has shown the holiness of Your love and Your will by her life of complete sanctity.

May You be praised and glorified by the heavens and the earth and by the sea and everything that is in it. You are worthy to be praised, glorified and exalted forever and ever. I now join my praises to all those who glorify, praise and bless You.

Father, today I want to renounce my sin of cursing. I am deeply ashamed, because my heart has become a fountain of indecent words, cursing and malediction. The curses from my tongue have struck You, Your saints and Your creatures like arrows. You wanted me to praise and to glorify You with my gift of speech, to speak words of consolation, words of wisdom, peace and healing to others. But I have abused the gift of speech through slander, insult and vilification.

Forgive me, Father. Purify my heart and let it become a fountain of consoling, kind and inspirational words for others and for You. I pray to You to heal me so that this decision I am making today will be permanent. I offer You all those who have cursed in my presence, starting with my elders who have scandalized me and have tempted me to evil. I pray also for those who swear, and who can no longer control their tongues, even though they want to do so. Deliver them from this evil habit. I pray for those who do not recognize the evil of cursing and swearing because their hearts have become indifferent. Bless them and awaken their hearts to holiness.

Protect all little children who are forced to listen to cursing, swearing, quarrels and impure language from their parents and their elders. Do not let their hearts be poisoned by what they hear. May they learn how to praise and glorify You. Father, enlighten me by the power of Your Spirit so that from this day on every word I speak will give You honor.

I pray for this nation and everyone in it who curses. Give us all the grace to know deep within our hearts how sacred You are and how exalted is Your holy name, so that we will never again be drawn to cursing.

Please, teach our hearts to sing Your praises joyfully. May we become a people who praise You and who celebrate Your wonderful deeds. Amen.

II

For Those Who Have Killed Innocent Life
(for cases of abortion)

People were bringing even infants to Him that
He might touch them, and when the disciples
saw this, they rebuked them. Jesus, however,
called the children to Himself and said, "Let
the children come to Me and do not prevent
them; for the kingdom of God belongs to such
as these. Amen, I say to you, whoever does
not accept the kingdom of God like a child
will not enter it."

Luke 18:15-17

Father in heaven, You are the Creator of
everything. You spoke the word, and everything
was created. We know all things are sustained by
Your will. Everything develops and grows under
the warmth of Your love. Thank You for creating
me and fashioning me in the womb of my mother.

May You be blessed, because You have given
all men the power to become co-creators with You.
May You be praised and glorified because You
fashioned the body of a woman to be able to
receive life, to sustain it, and to give birth to it.
Thank You for all who responsibly and joyfully
cooperate in the creation of life.

O Lord, I confess to You now that I have misused the gift which You entrusted to me. I confess that it is a great evil. I have killed life in its earliest stages. I have had an abortion. (Or) I have talked someone into an abortion. (Or) I have forced someone to have an abortion. I have killed innocent life. Forgive me. I realize that I have been misled by incorrect and false reasoning. I was searching for an excuse, because I didn't want more children, so I agreed to carry out this crime. I was ashamed to have more children. I was told that abortion was acceptable in the first trimester of pregnancy. I allowed myself to believe this lie, and I forgot that real human life begins at the moment of conception. I repent, Lord, because I have done this. I promise that from this day onwards I will seriously and responsibly preserve every conceived life. Please help me, Lord, with this decision. Pour Your love into my heart now, and strengthen me to carry out this decision.

Mary, Mother of the living and Mother of life, teach me to accept life as you accepted it. It was not easy for you to accept the baby Jesus. But you knew that the Creator of the universe wanted to be made incarnate and so you said, "Here I am Lord. I am Your servant." Teach me now, and through your intercession help me, please.

Lord, I pray to You now, with Mary, for all

fathers and mothers, adolescent boys and girls, doctors, and for all people. Enlighten us and help us to protect and to accept unborn life with love. I pray to You for all those who are now tempted to kill their unborn child. Send someone to encourage them and to help them choose life. Send me Lord, and give me the strength and the right words to encourage others to support life.

I pray for all women, wives, and young girls who are suffering intensely because they have had an abortion. May they come to You for forgiveness, peace, and love. I pray now in their name. Please answer my prayers. Forgive my nation for so many abortions. Do not let us destroy ourselves. Bless all pregnant women. Bless all unborn children. May their parents not be afraid of them. May they accept them. May parents accept their unborn children.

In this confession, I offer You all murders— of the unborn and the born. Reconcile us with You, Who live and give life constantly.

Jesus, You are the blessed fruit of the womb of Mary, the Virgin. You loved children and blessed them, and You taught us to love and accept children.

Bless all children. Receive into Your kingdom now, all those whose birth we have prevented.

May they all enjoy eternal life through You, with You, and in You, You Who are the source of life.

Jesus, You who were the victim of violence, forgive us our sins so that we can be happy with You in eternity. We ask this through Christ our Lord. Amen.

III
Forgive My Trespasses
*(For those who have known
lasting and destructive quarrels.)*

Where do the wars and where do the conflicts among you come from? Is it not from your passions that make war within your members? You covet but do not possess. You kill and envy but you cannot obtain; you fight and wage war. You do not possess because you do not ask. You ask but do not receive, because you ask wrongly, to spend it on your passions. Adulterers. Do you not know that to be a lover of the world means enmity with God? Therefore, whoever wants to be a lover of the world makes himself an enemy of God. Or do you suppose that the scripture speaks without meaning when it says, "The spirit that He has made to dwell in us tends toward jealousy?" But He bestows a greater grace; therefore, it says: "God resists the proud, but gives grace to the humble." So submit yourselves to God. Resist the devil, and he will flee from you. Draw near to God, and He will draw near to you. Cleanse your hands, you sinners, and purify your hearts, you of two minds. Begin to lament, to mourn, to weep. Let your laughter be turned into mourning and your joy into dejection.

Humble yourselves before the Lord and He will exalt you.

James 4:1-10

Be merciful, just as your Father is merciful. Stop judging and you will not be judged. Stop condemning and you will not be condemned. Forgive and you will be forgiven. Give and gifts will be given.

Luke 6:36-37

Then Peter approaching asked Him, "Lord, if my brother sins against me, how often must I forgive him? As many as seven times?" Jesus answered, "I say to you, not seven times but seventy-seven times."

Matthew 18:21-22

Father, in heaven, You are merciful and good. Your Son Jesus Christ teaches me to forgive every offense. I ask forgiveness for every way I have offended You and others. Jesus teaches me to forgive my enemies from my heart. If I do not forgive others, and if I do not seek forgiveness from them, then You cannot forgive me.

Father, thank You for offering forgiveness and a new beginning with You and with others. Thank You for never closing the door when someone knocks and asks for mercy.

May You be praised and glorified for Your mercy, which You have shown to me in the past and are ready to show me again. Jesus, teach me to know how to forgive, just as I wish to be forgiven. Strengthen my love, so that forgiveness and peace will never again be missing from my relationship with You and others.

Mary, you continuously call me to peace and to reconciliation. I know that you want me to start forgiving and to ask for forgiveness. Teach me to surrender to whatever your Son, and my Savior, wants from me.

Jesus, I now confess that it is difficult for me to forgive. This is why I have quarrels and misunderstandings with others and with You. I confess to You that envy, jealousy, gossip, harsh words and evil deeds flowed from my heart because I would not be reconciled. I have offended others, and others have offended me. My heart is wounded, and I have wounded others, because I would not forgive. Through my unforgivingness, I have damaged my life, my family, and the life of my community. I acknowledge that every time I am not reconciled with someone, I suffer greatly.

You know how hard it is for me to forgive. Therefore, I beg You, before I receive Your forgiveness through the priest in confession, give me the strength to forgive, with all my heart, everyone with whom I am not at peace, everyone from whom I am separated by a wall of hatred, envy, suspicion, jealousy, arrogance and pride. Give me the strength to embrace them all and to extend my hand to them joyfully in reconciliation. Forgive me, for in the past I did not take reconciliation seriously. I excused myself, blamed others, and believed that they should come and ask forgiveness because they offended me. I am sorry that many times selfishness and pride influenced my decisions, and I have not been humble and eager to make peace.

Forgive me. Purify my heart from all sinful relationships and from my dependency on people and things. Set me free to celebrate in joy and peace the power of Your mercy and forgiveness.

I pray, too, for all those whom I have offended. Give them the grace to forgive me also, so that the evil of unreconciliation and unforgiveness can be stopped. Father, through forgiveness may we become complete reflections of You.

I pray to You for all unreconciled families, where parents will not forgive their children, where children will not show mercy to their parents. May husbands and wives always have the strength to forgive one another, and to live together in peace. I pray to You for all those who are in danger of divorce, because they will not be reconciled to one another. I pray to You for all those who are separated from their spouses; may they be given the grace to reconcile. Help children of divorced parents to overcome their bitterness and their inability to forgive their parents. When parents start hating one another and refusing to forgive one another, they wound their children.

Look on all nations and systems of government which destroy peace because they do not honor You and do not have the strength to forgive others. Through our hands, extended in reconciliation, may peace come to all nations.

Queen of Peace, Mother of goodness, love and mercy, with your motherly goodness, intercede for your children who do not know how to obtain peace for the whole Church, and for every community within the Church. Through your intercession, may all Christian churches and all religions of the world be reconciled.

Dear Jesus, Your life revealed the Father's mercy to us and called us to be merciful and forgiving. As I meditate upon Your word, I pray to You for the necessary graces to be sent to the whole world. Let **peace** reign throughout the world. May everyone learn how to forgive the debts of others, just as, through You, Your Father forgives all our debts.

Jesus, I want to go out to the whole world to spread Your forgiveness. Send me Your Spirit, and inspire me and strengthen me. Amen.

IV
Neither Do I Condemn You

Father in heaven, thank You, because today I realize again how great are Your mercy and Your goodness. Thank You for the words of the priest that You sent to me in the sacrament of Confession, who said in Your name, "I absolve you from your sins. Go in peace." Now I sincerely want to bring this peace to my whole family and to the people with whom I live. From now on, I will witness to Your love by loving You above all else and by loving my neighbor as myself.

To those whom I have offended, I want to bring peace and joy every day through the way I live my life. I want to live every day full of gratitude to You. I want to be grateful to everyone who loves me. I want to notice and to acknowledge the smallest gift which is given to me through other people, so that I will be constantly grateful to You and to them.

I even give You thanks for all the good You will accomplish through me in the future. May everything I do give You glory and praise. You have not wanted to condemn me; rather You have enabled me to become an instrument of Your peace and love for the world. I now offer to You all those moments when I will be tested and even fall because of my weakness, and I ask Your help.

I offer to You now those moments in which my love will fail.

May Your love heal me and renew my whole life. I offer You my wounded heart. May negative feelings never dominate me again.

Give me the strength and the insight to find always the right words for others; words that will heal, strengthen, encourage, and teach. Help me never to condemn others. Rather, help me to pray for them and make sacrifices for them.

May the peace with which the priest sends me into the world after my confession always reign in my heart. For surely, these words have come to me from You, "Go in peace."

Oh Lord, through the intercession of Your beloved servant Mary, help me to become an instrument of Your peace and reconciliation.

Queen of Peace, Mother of beautiful love, teach me and all of your children how to love.

Dear Children! Hatred gives birth to dissensions and does not regard anyone or anything. I call you always to bring harmony and peace. Especially, dear children, in the place where you live, act with love. Let your only instrument always be love. By love turn everything into good which Satan desires to destroy and to possess.

Only that way will you be completely mine and I will be able to help you. Thank you for having responded to my call.

July 31, 1986

May my love grow and reach its fullness in eternity. Amen.

V
The Ten Commandments

1. I am the Lord your God, you shall not have strange gods before Me.

2. You shall not take the Name of the Lord your God in vain.

3. Remember to keep holy the Lord's Day.

4. Honor your father and mother.

5. You shall not kill.

6. You shall not commit adultery.

7. You shall not steal.

8. You shall not bear false witness against your neighbor.

9. You shall not covet your neighbor's wife.

10. You shall not covet your neighbor's goods.

VI
Rules for Living

I will believe in God and love Him with all my heart.

I will praise God and pray to Him.

I will celebrate the Eucharist on Sunday with God's people.

I will help care for our family and not expect my parents to do this alone.

I will take care of my health.

I will joyfully lend and share with others what I possess.

I will always speak the truth, and I will not disclose anyone's secrets.

I will faithfully perform my duties.

VII
Practical Example of How to Prepare for Confession

(What follows is the practical preparation for confession used in May 1986 during a night vigil with young people. This same format could be used during pilgrimages or spiritual retreats.)

Practical directions for the leader.

1. Before entering the Church turn off all the lights.

2. Darkness is meant to symbolize the soul in sin.

3. Have the Easter candle ready, as well as a candle for each believer, priest, and confessor.

4. In the silence, pay close attention to what you are feeling.

Sample Reflection

Brothers and sisters in Christ, many times we have lived in darkness. Knowing that we should have spread the light, we have spread darkness.

Many times we have spread hatred, knowing

that instead we should have spread love.

Many times we have killed hope and spread despair, knowing that we should have spread hope.

Often we have begun in darkness, and continued to live in darkness.

But now we are here because we want to cross the Red Sea. We have been living in darkness and slavery, and now we want to live in the light.

I do not know what is in your hearts. I can only imagine. Forgive me, please, for beginning by speaking to you about the existence of darkness in your hearts.

Maybe at this moment some of you feel like a person leaving the doctor's office where you have just learned that you are seriously ill. In your heart, you may feel sadness, pain, insecurity, and emptiness. But that is not the most important thing right now. If you feel the power of Jesus in your heart and body at this moment, then you should not despair. There is an answer. Jesus is with us. He came and brought the light. He said, **"I am the Light."**

Jesus, I do not want to remain in darkness. I want Your light to fill my life, my soul, and my heart. I want Your light to fill my family, and all my encounters with my neighbor. I want your light to fill my school, my studies, and my work. Jesus, I want to live in the light. You are offering Yourself to me as my light. I open my heart to You right now.

Jesus, in Your presence, I sincerely ask myself, "How am I living my life?" I want to examine my whole life before You. Help me to look honestly at my life under the light of Your love. I ask, "Where are You in my life, Jesus?"

Do I love God the Father before all else, as You want me to?

Do I love my neighbor? Do I appreciate the gifts You have given me?

Jesus, I ask these questions before You, in Your light. Help me to look honestly at the answers.

You want me to pray and to trust You. I ask now, "Have I been praying as You desire?"

Jesus, You want to feed me and to nourish me at Mass by meeting me in the Word and in the Eucharistic Bread. You have given these gifts to me. I ask myself now, how have I participated in the Holy Mass? Many times I have participated without devotion, and I have not really met You.

Jesus, in Your presence, I examine how I have used my tongue, my gift of speech. Have I praised You, glorified You, blessed You, or have I used my tongue to belittle Your Name, to use Your Name in vain, blaspheming and offending You?

Jesus, in Your presence, I ask myself how have I used cigarettes, alcohol, drugs, food? Have I indulged in them too much?

Jesus, in Your presence, I ask myself how have I used television, and newspapers? How have I used the precious time You have given me?

Jesus, have I obeyed You when You asked me to respect my body and soul and the body and soul of others? Have I cherished human life before and after birth?

Jesus, it is especially important for me to come before You now and ask myself how have I responded to Your call for me to love all people?

In Your presence I ask, what have I done with the plan You had for my life when You gave me gifts and asked that I serve You and others with them?

Lord, I ask all these questions and hope that through the power of Your Holy Spirit I will find the answers.

Let us remain in silence now and search for the answers. Let us listen to our heart. Truthfully, no one but God can really know us. Close your eyes now, and in silence listen for His voice. Through His light you are going to see the light.

For the leader

1. Ask everyone to renounce their sins.

2. Urge them to decide for the light.

3. Light the Easter candle.

4. Turn to the priests and give them candles and pray for them.

VIII
Sample Prayers

In the name of Jesus Christ I ask You;

Do you renounce sin?

Do you renounce selfishness and hatred?

Do you renounce all evil?

Do you renounce the influence of Satan?

(other possible questions)

Are you ready to accept Jesus Christ as your light? If you are ready to accept Jesus as your light, then, in your name I light this Easter candle. It is a sign of our risen Lord, Who was raised from the dead by the Father.

(To the priests) You, brother priests, I ask you in front of God's people, are you ready at this moment to be ministers of reconciliation, and to absolve sins in the name of the Lord? Are you ready to bring light and peace to the souls of God's children?

When you are ready to spread God's light, please come to the altar and light your candle from the main candle that represents Christ. Then go into the church which is in darkness, and carry your light. Be ready and wait with your light for those who are looking for you.

(As priests depart silently for their confessionals in the church, we pray for them.)

Lord Jesus Christ, I pray for my brother priests. Inflame their hearts with the power of Your love as they light their candles from Your candle. Help them to spread this light, and may they always guard this light.

Lord Jesus Christ, inspire these priests with Your Word, inspire them with Your Spirit, and help them in their ministry of reconciliation. Through them bring reconciliation and peace, and heal everything that has been destroyed and wounded by sin. Heal their hearts, Lord. Give them joy and peace. Bless all priests and all confessors who are so joyfully willing to serve their brothers and sisters, whom You redeemed with Your blood. Bless all priests who are tired and who are suffering.

(The leader turns to the faithful and prays for them as they approach the priests. After each confession and absolution, the penitent lights his candle from the candle his confessor is holding. This gesture is a symbol of receiving reconciliation and the ministry of reconcil-

*iation. Penance is then prayed while the penitent holds
the lighted candle. All this should be done with dignity.
Anyone present who is not receiving the sacrament of
Confession, should go to a priest and ask to be blessed,
and light his candle from the priest's candle.)*

I ask you now, dear brothers and sisters, are
you ready to approach the priests, confess your
sins, and light your candle from their candle?

Please come to the altar. Take a candle and
go to a priest. Ask him to bless you, and if you
want to confess your sins, do so. If you do not
want to go to confession at this time, tell the priest
what resolutions you made during your last
confession, and ask for his blessing to help you
fulfill those resolutions. Then light your candle,
so that new light will fill the church. With each
confession the light in the church will increase.

*(As the penitents approach to take a candle and
proceed to confession, the leader prays:)*

Lord Jesus Christ, I pray for my brothers and
sisters who are taking these unlighted candles and
going to the priests. As they meet with the priests,
may You come to meet Your children who are
looking for forgiveness and healing. May every
decision to repent be firm and constant.

Lord Jesus Christ, pour out the fullness of Your

grace on all those who are now coming to confession. May all darkness disappear from their hearts, their families, the Church and the world.

Mary, you are our Mother. You want us to be renewed and you are calling us to be renewed through reconciliation and conversion. You want us to embrace you just as you have embraced us. Intercede for us, your children, so that we will belong completely to you. Through your help, may we become the light of the world, and a new source of hope and peace, just as through God's power, you became the dawn of the new day.

We pray, Lord, send Your Spirit upon us. We join our prayers to those of Mary, Your humble servant, and ask You to enlighten our hearts, to pour joy and love into us, and to heal us completely. Through us, may Your Spirit heal the whole world.

(While the penitents are going to confession, it is good to sing some songs of forgiveness and mercy, or to read some biblical texts, explaining them through meditation.)

Perhaps your sins are overwhelming, very overwhelming, and at this moment your heart is condemning you. Do not be afraid, even if your heart is condemning you. The Lord God is bigger than your heart.

Whenever sin seems enormous, and because sin is enormous, the Lord has prepared an even greater grace, and as a result our hope can be greater.

Do not ask, "Lord, what am I going to receive when I let go of this sin, this mistake, this bad habit?" Do not ask, "Lord, what am I going to receive in return for leaving this sin?" The Lord is full of mercy, and He always gives more than we can ask or even desire. The Lord is pure love and mercy.

(Once the individual confessions are over, the leader asks everyone to stand and sing some Easter songs. After the songs, the candles are extinguished. Now their hearts have become new lighted candles, and they will carry this light into the world.)

Dear friends, brothers and sisters, we began this celebration in darkness. We admit that often we have begun our day and then continued to work and to live in the darkness of sin. Now we know that it is possible to live in the light. Thank You, Jesus Christ, because You are the Light. We adore You and we bless You. You are our hope, our love, and our salvation.

(Renewal of Baptismal promises.)

In the name of the Church, I now ask all of you who have gone to confession, and are ready to go into the world:

Do you believe in God the Father almighty, creator of heaven and earth?

Do you believe in Jesus Christ our Savior and Redeemer?

Do you believe that love is stronger than hate?

Do you believe that light is stronger than darkness?

Do you believe that it is possible to surrender your life to God's will?

Do you accept Mary as your Mother?

Do your consecrate yourself to Mary now with your whole being?

Before you go into the world receive this blessing:

In the name of the Father, Who is your Creator, in the name of Jesus Christ, Who is your Redeemer and Savior, and in the name of the Holy Spirit,

Who is your Sanctifier, may the fullest blessing come to each of you.

May you be blessed with peace, joy, love, hope, fellowship, and forgiveness. May you be blessed with light and goodness. May you be blessed with a spirit of prayer and a spirit of obedience to God's will. May you be blessed with inner strength, so that you will be able to withstand all temptations. May you be protected from every evil. May you be blessed with the fullness of God's life. May you live in grace, and remain blessed forever. Peace be with you. Amen.

(Encourage the penitents to take their candle home so they may always be reminded of the moment of their decision for Christ, and their call to prayer, to love, and to forgiveness. Encourage them to pray before that candle.)

IX
Monthly Confession
Days of Reconciliation

The man who thinks he is safe must be careful
that he does not fall. The trials that you have
had to bear are no more than people normally
have. You can trust God not to let you be tried
beyond your strength, and with any trial He
will give you a way out of it and the strength
to bear it.

I Corinthians 10:12-13

According to statements of the visionaries, the
Blessed Mother recommends monthly confession
as a means to help us grow in peace. In the parish
community of Medjugorje, the first Friday,
Saturday, and Sunday are days devoted to
reconciliation. In response to this call to monthly
confession, we often hear the question, "Why do
we have to go to confession so frequently?" In
light of what we know about the rules of spiritual
living, it is easy to understand this call for monthly
reconciliation.

Our need for the sacrament of Reconciliation
is connected not only to our need to confess what
we have done wrong, but even more to our need
to grow in love, peace, mercy, and forgiveness.
Even if we can say that we have not sinned, we

are not exempt from the need to celebrate the sacrament of Reconciliation. The sacrament of Reconciliation is meant to be a celebration and a joyful meeting with God which brings healing and a renewed life. Whoever practices monthly confession in this spirit will begin to understand the laws of spiritual growth. They will begin to grasp the purpose of meeting with the priest. It will become easier for them to be committed to personal growth. They will become more sensitive to the dangers of sin, and eventually they will be healed of the wounds received through sin.

We might compare this process of reconciliation, this coming to know the interior of man's soul, with looking into a room. If we enter a person's room and look at the pictures and other objects, we begin to understand what that person likes, what is important to him, even what he has set his heart on. It is the same when we look into the soul. When we bring divine light into the soul on a regular basis, everything in the soul is eventually put in order, and it becomes easier to discover even the smallest imperfections in the soul. Dependencies are stopped, and all the negative influences of the world in which we live are resisted much more effectively. The more difficult the circumstances in which we find ourselves, the greater our need for interior housecleaning and healing. All the events of the world shape our soul and our experiences, and cause our fears, insecurities and tensions. It is all too easy to accommodate ourselves to evil and to negative influences, and to lose our commitment to what is good, holy and beautiful, and even to lose our belief in love, peace, truthfulness and friendship. Monthly confession is a great help for removing all impurities and sins immediately, and preventing the negative effects of sin.

Each one of us radiates what we carry in our hearts. If we carry good, then we radiate good. If we carry love, we will radiate love, just as we will radiate hatred when we carry hatred in our hearts.

This helps us to understand how our sins affect other people. Perhaps we can now realize that monthly confession is meant to protect us from evil, as well as to cleanse us from the evil already accumulated in our hearts.

If we work in a factory full of poisonous materials, or in any situation which endangers our lives, we will obviously take precautions to protect ourselves. If we do not protect ourselves in these situations, then we are acting irresponsibly.

In today's world, we do not need to judge one another's spiritual health, just as we do not need to judge a person who is physically sick. On the contrary, we need to understand one another, and help to heal one another. But we also need to protect ourselves from the sickness of the world caused by sin, so that we can become spiritually strong and help others to become spiritually healthy also.

According to the experiences of the prayer groups in Medjugorje, it is also clear that the Blessed Mother sometimes advises weekly confession. She has encouraged this during the weeks of special preparation for the feasts of Christmas, Easter, and Pentecost, and on other special occasions.

Mary, as our Mother, wants nothing else for her children than to see us receive healing, and become spiritually healthy so that we can always live in peace.

X
Annual Confession

We all know that one of the Church's commandments is that we must confess our sins at least once a year and receive Communion during the Easter season. There are reasons for this teaching of the Church, but we will not go into them at this time. One thing, however, is certain. Many believers are committed to confessing their sins no more than once a year.

If we compare our spiritual lives to the life of our body, and sin to sickness in the body, perhaps we can begin to understand how dangerous confessing only once a year is for us. Obviously, when our body is sick, we look for a doctor right away. How sad if the doctor tells us that we have come too late, the sickness has spread, and can no longer be stopped. How hopeless this diagnosis sounds in the ears of the sick patient.

When we sin, and through sin destroy ourselves and others, we should not postpone confessing these sins. The longer we carry spiritual wounds and tensions, and the longer they remain in our soul, the more destructive they become. Eventually these wounds will lead to the death of our spiritual life. It is dangerous to keep them inside, waiting for a yearly confession. Believers who do this do not realize that sin should be confessed immediately, as soon as possible, so that we can be set free and be open to the grace of reconciliation and forgiveness.

The person who does not go to confession immediately after sinning seriously gradually loses his sensitivity to sin. This is a dangerous condition for each of us, as well as for the community or family where the sin has been committed. This has a deadly effect on the community where we live, and destroys love and peace and every other spiritual fruit. We should not remain in this condition. We should not wait for yearly confession, just as we would not wait to care for a wound which will not heal itself, and with time will become more infected and poisonous.

If we are living this way, we are, in effect, saying that we are good Christians; but, in truth, we are really no more committed to stopping evil than those who do not know God.

XI
General Confession

Certain confessions are known as general confession, or the confession of all the sins of our entire life. During a routine confession of our sins, we mention when we last made a confession, so that the priest has a better grasp of our spiritual condition. There are also occasions when we may make a general confession. This means that on a particular occasion we confess whatever sins we have committed throughout our whole life. This general confession may be made at various times: for example, when we enter religious life, before ordination, before the taking of a vow, before marriage, before entering the armed services, during a retreat or pilgrimage, or before any other important event in our lives.

There are definitely times when it is beneficial to make a general confession of the sins of our whole life. But this should never be done because we think that God has not forgiven us, or because in a past confession we did not tell the priest everything, or because we forgot to mention certain things. Even if we did not confess everything in a previous confession, out of fear or shame, this is not a reason to make a general confession.

A general confession is helpful, and recommended as a way to grow spiritually, and to understand our whole life better. It is an excellent way to heal the wounds which have festered in us because of sin. Although it is usually not necessary to go back and disturb old wounds, if an area of our lives comes into our thoughts repeatedly, or even into our dreams, then it is good to confess this area again, to pray for it and to ask for healing.

As we confess the details of our sins and mistakes, we should never be afraid or scrupulous before God. Scrupulosity is inconsistent with God's mercy and love. If we are experiencing this condition in our spiritual lives, it is very important to be obedient to the advice of the priest. Such problems might come from mental sickness, or from deep fears which have evolved from our relationships with other people, and now we are transferring these fears onto God. Problems with scruples might also come from attacks of the devil. If the cause of the scrupulosity seems to arise from mental sickness, then the priest should help the penitents, and send them to professional people for further healing.

Confession is an occasion to call on God's love and mercy, and there is no reason for fear even when we discover that our past confessions have been imperfect. Confession is a special occasion of grace for the life of the soul, and it should bring us joy. Through confession, God is giving us a new beginning, and opening the way for peace and reconciliation.